P9-DND-817

The Super Baruba Success Book

for under-achievers, over-expecters, and other ordinary people

The Super Baruba Success Book

for under-achievers, over-expecters, and other ordinary people

BRAD WILCOX

Bookcraft
Salt Lake City, Utah

Library of Congress Catalog Card Number: 79-53050
ISBN O-88494-372-0

First Printing, 1979

Lithographed in the United States of America
PUBLISHERS PRESS
Salt Lake City, Utah

To my parents,
my two best friends

Contents

Foreword

As Brad Wilcox tells the reader immediately, Bookcraft invited him to write this book. The catalyst for this invitation was his article published in the *New Era* magazine and his first-place award in the nationwide youth writing contest conducted by *Guideposts* magazine.

Those achievements, a high level of attainment for an eighteen-year-old, were merely the tip of the iceberg, we discovered. But much more important for our purposes than the extent of his accomplishments was whether at his age the experience of his upward pull could give help to others on the road, whatever their age. When we met Brad Wilcox the answer turned out to be an emphatic yes.

As the book portrays, the key for the author is — Try. Hardly a revolutionary concept! Rather obvious, in fact, or so one would suppose were it not for the fact that ninety-nine out of a hundred people don't believe in it, to judge by their actions or inactions. Brad Wilcox combines this somewhat abused principle with one not so apparent. Ignoring the more popular and vociferous claims that personal success lies in being the winner (of which there can be only one at a time), he maintains that instead it consists in correctly shaping one's course, setting goals along it, achieving them, then setting progressively more difficult ones. Simply put, that's success — in attainable, bite-size pieces. And simply put, persistent effort — *trying*, that is — will attain it.

It helps too if you have talent, wide-ranging interests, and a positive approach to life, as the author has. Besides his successes with the written word, both locally and nationally, he has competed successfully in several speech contests and was second-place winner in the 1979 *Reader's Digest* Boy Scouts of America National Public Speaking Contest. Recipient of national honors also in drama and music, he has appeared in many theatrical presentations in the West, he has performed on national tours with the BYU Young Ambassadors and in the musical "My Turn On Earth," and he toured Europe in 1976 as one of Utah's representatives in the All-American Bicentennial Choir. In 1978-1979 he was National Youth Representative on the National Executive Board of the Boy Scouts of America. The list is lengthy. Active in the LDS Church, in June 1979, while this book was being produced, he left home to serve as a missionary in the Chile Viña del Mar Mission.

Brad Wilcox is quick to acknowledge the help from others which made his progress possible. He is equally quick to recognize errors along the way, and his absorbing and humorous book recounts many of these stepping-stones against the background of his ten principles governing the kind of success we can all achieve.

The author was eighteen when he wrote the first draft for this book. Bookcraft offers his book in the conviction that it provides not only good reading but valuable help and encouragement to persons of all ages.

THE PUBLISHER

Acknowledgments

I am grateful to Vermont Harward, a sensitive teacher, who organized an entire creative writing class for fourth graders because of the interest of just one boy named Brad.

I acknowledge with appreciation also the sustained interest and encouragement of Margo and Wayne Wilcox, Steve Perry, and Beth Duering; and of George Bickerstaff, who believes in young people, believes in me, and believed that this idea of a book could become a reality.

I express thanks to Chloe Vroman who, in the course of shepherding this manuscript to completion, has graduated from a teacher I admire to a teacher I love.

Finally, I am grateful to my mother for the use of her poetry and articles, and for typing and checking the manuscript; and to both her and my father for their never-failing encouragement.

1

I Think He Can Write "Y's"

"I challenge you to write a book!" Mr. Bickerstaff, Senior Editor of Bookcraft, leaned forward across his paper-strewn desk. I was stunned. "But, look, Hugh Nibley I'm not. George Durrant I'm not."

"Brad Wilcox you are." He clasped his fingers and spoke earnestly. "No other person in the world has had your individual experiences and can relate them in exactly your way."

I stopped listening. My mind was going off in eight directions. I sat uncomfortably on the comfortable chair in the editor's office feeling overwhelmed.

"Me, write a book?" I stammered to myself. "I'm only eighteen!" As though I were listening to a radio, I tuned back to the man facing me.

"Brad, you have something to tell people — something important."

I smiled as naturally as I could. "Me?" I asked in astonishment, forcing a weak laugh.

"Yes, you. I read with much interest your short stories in the *New Era* magazine and in *Guideposts*. You have learned a valuable principle at a young age. What do you say? Will you take my challenge?"

I looked at the stacks of manuscripts on the shelf across the office from me. "But what can I say that hasn't already been said a thousand and one times before?" I asked. "Mr. Bickerstaff, our family just got my dad a book of great quotations for his birthday, one thousand and one pages of well-stated eternal truths."

"So it's one thousand and two; it will be coming from you. Brad, there are readers out there who would like to know what you have learned. You have something to say, so here's your chance to say it." He pushed his chair slightly away from the desk and started to rise, bringing our interview to a close. I stood and shook his outstretched hand.

"Thank you very much."

"Now, Brad," he said, still clasping my hand, "accept my challenge. Don't let this opportunity slip by."

As I stood there I suddenly realized that my thinking was all wrong. I could have kicked myself. "Only eighteen!" I've always believed that young people could accomplish anything if they were given the opportunity. Why was I hesitating? Here was an opportunity — an incredible, unbelievable chance to prove my theory.

But still I rationalized. A book! In all my wondering about the purpose of our meeting I had never imagined that I would be asked to write a book. Again I surveyed the pile of manuscripts across the office. Could I do it? Realistically, could I produce anything more than ten pages long that would be worthwhile?

"There's one way to find out," I told myself. "You have to try."

Mr. Bickerstaff shifted to break the silence.

"I will do it. I will write this book. Thank you, Mr. Bickerstaff." He smiled and walked me to the lobby.

"I'll check back with you soon," I promised. I waved and marched semi-confidently out of the building toward the parking lot. "Maybe I do have something to say. Maybe I can write this book," I kept chanting to myself. I knew it would be a totally new experience for me, hard work, but fun, too. "I must try," I thought. "After all, whether it is ever published or not, I will be involved, improving my skills and abilities and preparing myself for other challenges. Okay, it is decided. I will take this rare opportunity and say what I need to say."

I drove in silent contentment for several miles, when out of the back of my mind came a thought the size of a diesel truck. "What *do* I have to say?" That question flattened me without stopping to see what it had hit. Could I phone Mr. Bickerstaff and ask, "What *do* I have to say?"

Naturally my family wondered about my interview. No matter how I tried to stall, the question kept surfacing, "What, exactly, are you going to write about?" Why hadn't I thought of this myself before so dramatically accepting Mr. Bickerstaff's challenge? With as much mystery and nonchalance as I could fake, I finally replied, "I'll tell you later."

The following day I wandered from class to class in a mental paralysis. "What do I have to say?" The question repeated itself over in my mind like a TV re-run — until English class, that is. As soon as the themes were passed back, the only thing my mind zeroed in on was the red 71 in the corner of my paper.

Mrs. Vroman's white chalk scratched — 85, 85, 83. I cringed with every stroke and stared patiently ahead. She continued her usual listing of all thirty-three theme paper scores on the warped chalkboard. I lowered my head to look again at the folded corner of my paper. Seventy-one! The number stuck out like a tenor in a ward choir. How come so low? I couldn't understand what I had done wrong. "It was a good theme," I thought. Carefully covering the score with my American Literature book, I studied the paper again. There were so many corrections it looked as if someone had stabbed the poor thing and left it bleeding to death. "Where is your thesis statement?" "New thought, new paragraph." "Check misspelled words."

I looked up just as Mrs. Vroman finished. There was my seventy-one, and I figured it was good for a B, at least. "Fifty and below, F." Mrs. Vroman slashed a long horizontal line across the list just above fifty. Sixty-five and below, D." Again the chalk slashed.

Desperately figuring where my seventy-one fit into this scheme, I thought, "That means. . . ." And at the same moment her voice confirmed, "Seventy-five and below, C." My writing wasn't even worth a C plus, it was just a C — average, mediocre. The bell rang, and Mrs. Vroman finished. Slowly I joined the herd of students funneling down B wing. I opened the old locker, grabbed my scriptures, and buried the theme deep under a half-finished history project.

I shuffled toward the seminary building. Class began with the usual song and prayer. Then a girl got up to present the devotional, and — wouldn't you know it? — her subject was "We preach perfection but practice mediocrity." I slumped lower and lower with every syllable. "Too many of us are willing to settle for the C when we should strive for the A."

After class I hurried to the library and stationed myself before the school's oversized dictionary. "M — medieval, medina." There it was: "mediocre — of middle quality, ordinary. Mediocrity, comes from the Latin word 'mediocris' meaning 'half way up the mountain.' "

So perhaps mediocrity wasn't all that bad — so long as it wasn't the goal. Mediocre is simply a point you have reached. It doesn't mean that's as far as you can go. It only means that's as far as you have come. Halfway there and on the way up doesn't seem such a bad record. I resented the seminary statement, "Don't be mediocre. . . ." In my mind, the only way to reach perfection was to climb the mountain, and I was halfway there!

I grabbed my books and headed into the near-empty hall, triumphant with my new understanding. I was ready to go home. As I passed Mrs. Vroman's room I remembered that I had forgotten to leave the American Literature book, one of a classroom set. So I stepped into the room, to find Mrs. Vroman deep in serious conversation with a friend of mine.

"Excuse me." They both turned toward me, unsmiling. Mrs. Vroman seemed unusually somber. "I'm sorry to interrupt. I forgot to leave this book."

"Just put it on the shelf, Brad." Across an empty desk between them she leaned toward him and they continued their conversation.

I slipped to the back of the room as unobtrusively as I could. Then I overheard the words "dropping out." I froze. I couldn't believe what I was hearing.

"What are you going to do with your time?" she asked.

"Nothing." His deep voice was harsh.

I knew of other people who had dropped out of high school to go to work, or to attend institutes that didn't require high school diplomas, but to do nothing. . . !

"I'm sick of being forced to do things other people think I

should do. I used to think I could handle it, but I can't and I don't have to. It's my own choice and I'm choosing out. I'm sick of not getting anywhere — sick of being mediocre!"

The word was so fresh on my mind I couldn't resist injecting, "That's halfway up the mountain. You're on your way up." I started forward in the room. "If you stop now you might start slipping back."

"How did you get into this?" he interrupted, and continued pacing from desk to window. When I finished he stopped, stared at me and barked, "Look, Brad, I can't do what everybody expects me to do, all right?"

Mrs. Vroman stretched out her arm as if to calm the situation, and said, "It doesn't matter if you can or if you can't, only that you try."

Usually when she said that I'd think, "Trite — cliche — same old line." But suddenly, for some reason, I realized that one of Satan's most powerful tools against me is making important things sound insignificant and petty. "I love you." "Thank thee for this food." "The gospel is true." "It doesn't matter if you can or can't, only that you try."

The words rang through my mind — "only that you try, that you try." For a moment, time stopped for me. With Mrs. Vroman's words I was transported miles and years away to another classroom, another friend, and another teacher.

"Mr. Wilcox," she said (she always called me Mr. Wilcox), "this is a new friend in our class." I gave him a great, gap-tooth second-grade smile, but he didn't smile back. Slowly Mrs. Shuey led the way to his desk across the room, introducing him to other classmates on the way. I don't remember his name. I don't think I knew it even back then.

He was late beginning his second-grade year because his family had just arrived in Addis Ababa, the capital city of Ethiopia. It was my second year in Africa, where my father was a professor at the Haile Selassie I University. As with any school, there were all kinds of kids from all kinds of families at the American Community school, but this new boy seemed different from any I had ever met. He didn't look different, but after a few days in our class I sensed a strangeness about him. Though we crowded around him at lunchtime, he didn't talk much. When the rest of us eagerly burst through the classroom doorway for recess, he lingered before coming to the playground.

It was about a week after he came that we began to learn the magical art of cursive writing. As I look at my casual-to-sloppy handwriting now, I pride myself that in second grade, at least, I had the neatest, most legible penmanship in class. Because my name Bradley ends in *y* I had grown to love the letter and had practiced it at home. So when the day came for writing cursive *y*'s at school I finished my practice page in a hurry. Triumphantly I rushed to present the finest *y* paper in the world for Mrs. Shuey's praise. "Mr. Wilcox," she whispered, "you wrote this letter so well, I wonder if you will be my assistant teacher until the bell rings." I was honored to follow her to the desk of my quiet classmate.

"Brad is going to help you learn to write *y*," she explained. I sat next to him and began, "It's easy, you just go up to the middle line, then down and around like a tail, and it's a *y*."

He simply sat. Not belligerently or angrily or anything, he just sat. "It's not that hard, honest. You just go up to the middle line and —" the bell interrupted my lesson. He still stared blankly ahead. "We'll work on *y*'s tomorrow, okay?" I volunteered. Again, no response. Only an emptiness I felt but can't describe. We were dismissed. With my Donald Duck lunchbox in hand, I waved to him and ran for my bus.

Every day during cursive writing I showed my *y*'s, but he rarely even picked up his pencil. One day a man came into our room. The boy gathered his things and they left together.

"Where is he going?" I asked.

Mrs. Shuey stood near the window watching them cross the playground. "He's going to get some special help." I stared in astonishment to see tears drop onto a set of papers in her hands.

"Don't cry, Mrs. Shuey, I think he can write *y*'s."

"Mr. Wilcox." She turned and leaned down. "It doesn't matter that he can or that he can't, only that he try." She tightened her hold on my small shoulders as if to emphasize what she was about to tell me. "For some reason, that boy has given up. The only way we grow and progress is to try, and he isn't trying."

Mrs. Shuey patted my shoulders now. "Do you understand, Mr. Wilcox?"

"Yes," I said. I didn't really understand, but I was in danger of missing my bus. "See you tomorrow, Mrs. Shuey."

Now, as a senior in high school, I finally grasped the full import of Mrs. Shuey's profound statement those years ago.

"Nobody cares if you try, only if you win," my friend was saying. His words shook me back to the reality of the moment.

I stepped forward. "That's not true."

"That's easy for you to say, Brad," he blurted. I could tell he was fighting to hide tears. "You get *A*'s, you have trophies. You're even a student officer."

"Do you think that matters?" I asked.

Waving his hands dramatically, he mimicked, "Do you think that matters?"

I had thought I knew him so well. "Trophies are outdated a week after you get them," I went on. "Honors and grades are just measurements of growth as you try and then try again. Sure I've won contests, and I've lost contests, too."

"Look —" he started to interrupt.

Determined to be heard, I continued: "Winning's great. Losing's hard, but the happiness is in the trying. Fulfillment is in the trying, don't you see?"

My friend backed to the wall and stared angrily out of the window. It had begun to rain. The three of us stood in silence for almost a minute.

"Mrs. Vroman, just sign my release."

My heart sank. I had thought I knew him well. We had been biology partners. He sat by me in algebra. We always laughed together in the hall or lunchroom. Reluctantly, a very concerned teacher signed the paper.

I was ashamed of myself. Why hadn't I been more aware? I had no idea he was feeling this way. What could I say? Why wouldn't he listen? He snatched the paper and strode from the room.

"See ya," I offered weakly. No response. Just the finality of a banging door.

Mrs. Vroman walked slowly toward me. "For some reason that boy has given up. The only way we grow and progress is to try, and he isn't trying anymore. Do you understand, Brad?" How strange. The words sounded identical. Without turning to look at her, I folded my arms and let my mind slip back again to the American Community School. "Do you understand, Mr. Wilcox?"

"Yes," I whispered, "I do. This time I really do."

Beyond Mrs. Vroman, through the fogged window, I glimpsed my friend walking away from the campus, tugging at his coat collar in the cold. Surely there was *something* I could have done.

"Goodnight, Mrs. Vroman."

"Goodnight, Brad. Drive carefully in this rain."

I picked up my books and headed out into B wing. "Why should I care?" I asked myself. "It's none of my business anyway." But inside, my mind was helplessly swirling.

"We all have to learn for ourselves. I can't make him be happy. No one can be forced to compete with himself. I can't force him to try." I fought a silent battle.

"Can't he see how much he has going for him?" I used to wonder how I could pay Heavenly Father back for all the good things in my life. Within myself I gave thanks for blessings I appreciated, and pledged to show my gratitude the only way I can, by taking full advantage of every opportunity to be the best I can be. To try. I wanted to reach out and give this same challenge to my friend, but he was gone.

My old car looked abandoned in the student parking lot, an island in the sea of fresh puddles. "Mr. Bickerstaff was right," I thought. "I do have something to say!"

2

Please Help Me Win First Place

"Try!" Admittedly this is good advice. But it seems that most good advice tends to wash in and out of my mind, along with brothers' birthdays, license plate numbers, and every answer I was just sure I knew before I sat down to take the A.C.T. Perhaps the reason I resist absorbing good advice from others is not that I disbelieve it, or even disagree with it. It's easy to accept advice in theory. The difficulty arises in putting that advice into practice.

"Try," we are told. We are expected to produce an end, yet are left ignorant of the means. It is like the time my brother Chris asked me to play a game of chess with him, but somehow forgot to tell me the game rules. The question, then, is not, Should I try? Most of us would agree on that point. The question is, How? How do I try?

As I climb that mountain that stands between me and perfection, I can follow a basic and complete set of rules given to me by the Lord himself. He knows that to command, "Be ye therefore perfect. . . ." is not enough. He commands and then explains how to reach perfection through biblical commandments, and by modern revelation through living prophets.

For me to write about the importance of trying, and stop there, would be unfair and worthless. So in these chapters I hope you'll discover "Brad Wilcox's Ten Total Baruba Supreme Trying Steps." (That's an official-sounding title designed to make you think that these steps have been yanked out of some sure-fire, five-inch-thick textbook and are therefore infallible. Actually, they are a few steps which I've been asked to yank out of my one-inch-thick eighteen-year life.) Perhaps, somehow, in some story, on some page, you'll be able to identify with me.

One of my favorite fairy tales was about the boy who had been given some magic shoes. Once he had them on his feet he could ford huge rivers with ease, or clear entire mountain ranges with one giant stride. Sometimes I wish there were magic shoes for me in my own comfortable size. Then I could take giant strides toward my goals and jump easily over mountains of adversity and opposition with no effort. But this doesn't seem to be Heavenly Father's way. In my life so far I haven't found any shortcuts. Any steps I've taken have been baby steps up the mountain of perfection. Sure, there will always be moments when I leap forward, but there will also be moments when I'm swept backward. That's life. We lose some, we win some.

I've always liked what Rudyard Kipling said in his poem "If," where he tells us we must "meet with Triumph and Disaster and treat those two imposters just the same." How well I know that!

"I would that ye should be perfect even as I or your Father who is in heaven is perfect" (3 Nephi 12:48). As children of God we have the potential of rising to his perfection. But I can never reach such perfection unless I'm encouraged and guided to it by Christ and the Father, who are perfect. Therefore, in my life the first step to trying is *prayer*.

When I made this my first step I was encouraged to find that after God expelled Adam and Eve from the Garden of Eden his first recorded instruction to them was to worship the Lord (Moses 5:5). And through the world's entire history we have been counselled "that men ought always to pray." (Luke 18:1) (And Brother Willis thought I slept through his Sunday School lesson on all this!)

"Behold, I stand at the door and knock; if any man hear my voice and open the door, I will come into him and will sup with him and he with me." All my life I've heard Revelation 3:20 and never understood that prayer is my passage toward unity with Deity. Through this communication I can gain security in the knowledge that God will strengthen and protect me as I try to better myself.

You may be thinking, "Now hold it right there, Brad. Is this a book about prayer or a book about trying?" For the longest time I told myself that the two don't go together. That is where I was wrong. With this unity, we can try with total faith in Heavenly Father and in ourselves. Trying and praying must go together. The mistake I was making when I was younger was confusing trying with winning. "I've worked hard," I prayed, "so please help me win first place."

It was the Western Regionals of the *Reader's Digest* Boy Scouts of America National Public Speaking Contest. I rubbed my sweating palms up and down on my pant leg. My number was called. It was my turn to speak.

I stood and smiled calmly. Inside I frantically prayed. "This is it, God. Help me to win it." Slowly I walked to the front of the auditorium and positioned myself.

As I waited for the timekeeper's signal I surveyed the large audience. Everyone's attention was riveted on me. Again I smiled. Under my controlled facade my legs were shaking like jackhammers. I saw my family, each one beaming. My father winked a "good luck." But I wasn't depending on luck. I had worked. I deserved this. Today was the big day, the moment I would qualify for the national contest in Washington, D.C. My family had come with me all the way to San Francisco for this very moment. "I'm not going to let them down," I assured myself.

The timer flashed the card and I began my well-rehearsed speech. It flowed simply and naturally. Words leapt from mind to mouth. The audience was with me completely. They listened and laughed exactly in the right places. The final minute ticked off the timer's stopwatch and I built to my triumphant last line. "I explored within and discovered" — I paused — "me."

Applause rang through the auditorium. I walked confidently to my seat. "That's the best I've ever done it," I thought. The excitement of victory was already racing through my whole body. My face was flushed. I listened to subsequent contestants only enough to feel secure in the knowledge that I had done better than they. Otherwise I sat there trying out dreams of the all-expense trip. I could see myself already on the steps of the White House, Washington, D.C. Wow! I had worked hard, I had earned it, and now I knew it was mine.

After a short lunch break the judges made their decision. Everyone began to file back into the seats. The master of ceremonies gave his thank-you-to-everyone-and-all-the-contestants-were-great speech and started to announce the awards. "Sixth place. . . ." "Thank you Heavenly Father," I prayed. "Thank you for helping me win."

"Third place. . . ." While I was thinking of what I might say when I accepted the trophy, loudly and clearly I heard, "Second place, Brad Wilcox." The words burned through me like a laser beam.

Mom nudged my arm. I stood slowly and walked, zombie-like, to the stage, where I accepted the certificate and took my place with the others.

"Congratulations," the girl next to me offered. I just nodded. I couldn't make a sound come. Second place? Why? Didn't I have the best speech? This wasn't right!

I glared at the words on my certificate — "second place." Heavenly Father had neither heard nor answered my prayer. I bit my lip defiantly. I had done all I could do. I had really tried and he had let me down. Right then on that stage, wallowing in self-pity and hurt pride, I decided, "Trying and prayer don't mix."

It took me days and weeks to get over the disappointment I felt. I realize, now that I have formulated my steps of trying, that I had done everything wrong from step one on. But at the time I couldn't see that. I only knew that if Heavenly Father wasn't going to answer my prayers I wouldn't pray; so I didn't.

Then one day in the library during English I read Mark Twain's explanation of this trap, in his story "The War Prayer." The story is about a country at war. The setting is a small town the day before the battalions leave for the front. The church is full of people, all praying for their country's victory.

In Twain's unique way, the story continues with a heavenly messenger entering the church and quietly moving up the main aisle. The messenger proceeds to explain that "as you pray for the blessing of rain upon your crop, you may be working a curse upon your brother's crop that does not need rain and could be injured by it." Noting the bewilderment of the congregation, he puts it even more clearly. "When we pray for our victory we are praying for another's defeat." While that congregation prayed for the lives of their sons, they were offering unspoken prayers that the people they were fighting would lose, and that the enemy would lie dead, murdered; that widows and orphans would wander homeless, hungry and cold through their then-desolated wasteland. This they prayed with humble hearts in "the spirit of love of Him who is the source of love. . . ."

Even after it was put so plainly, the congregation dismissed Mark Twain's messenger as a lunatic "because there was no sense in what he said." I closed the book. "How foolish these people were," I thought. "Can't they see that simple truth?" Then I thought of myself. My face reddened as I realized how foolish I was being. Each time I pray to win a trophy, win the office, or win the game, I am also offering an unspoken prayer for someone else's defeat.

"Please help me win first place." How selfish I had been in San Francisco. It would have been so much wiser to ask for the strength and determination to earn it. As I was trying I was forgetting to put myself in the shoes of others. Every other contestant too had worked hard and wanted that trip as much as I did. How did I know that every other contestant had not also been praying, and how did I know that the one who won the first place trophy had not worked and prayed harder than any of us?

Rather than stepping on others as I climb, I must honestly help others. After all, wouldn't heaven be a lonely place with only Heavenly Father and me? It's human nature to pray for victory. But wouldn't it be better to pray, instead, to do my best?

"But I did do my best," I rationalized in the same way I had for weeks. "I was the top speaker in the competition. But I was still judged second place." I remembered how hurt I felt when the winner was announced. I couldn't face anyone. Now, while I sat in the library with Twain's story in front of me, another of my mistakes became apparent. When the places were announced I should have realized that the judges

I was dealing with were people; people with individual tastes and with their own free agency. I was the best in *my* opinion. Those judges listened and decided that another young man had a little more of what they were looking for. That's their prerogative. Here's how Mr. Ray B. Jones, my high school drama coach and good friend, explained it to me:

"When you go shopping for lettuce," he said, "when you have lettuce in your mind and lettuce is what you want to eat, as fresh and sweet as the carrots look you still want lettuce. Even if the carrots are on sale, you went into the store to buy lettuce." As well as I spoke during the contest, I was a carrot and the judges wanted lettuce.

Next time, because I am dealing with free-thinking human beings who make mistakes, I hope I'll be able to do everything I can do to prepare and then pray that others will be fair, honest and sensitive. "Next time," I resolved, as I sat in the quiet of the library, "I will also pray for the ability to be exactly that, if I'm ever in the position of judging a contestant or any child of God."

As I said at the beginning of this chapter, the question is not, Should I? The question is, How? How do I pray? David was a small friend who has long since moved out of the rental across the street from our house. He and I were in fourth grade together. David had never gone to Primary, or church for that matter, until that year. Every week I'd stop by the small apartment and pick up David, and we'd walk together through the large orchards and fields to the chapel. The weekly walks were a good time to talk about school, home, the next vacation, or how to solve world problems, and to float wood chips to China in the irrigation ditch.

One day after Primary we started our trek home. The class activity had gone a little overtime, so we were starting out later than usual. As we entered the cherry orchard, David walked a little behind me, stirring up the freshly fallen leaves with a stick he carried. I was busily dodging evening shadows, hopping from one sunspot to another, when David piped up, "I'm sorry I didn't say the prayer. Really."

I turned and looked at him. The autumn breeze blew freely through his thin blonde hair. "Oh, I don't care," I smiled. "You don't have to tell me you're sorry."

"Well, when Mrs. . . . I mean Sister Adams asked me to say the closing prayer I was going to — I mean, I wanted to. I just don't know how. I never have. Nobody in my family prays." By now David was walking at my side.

I laughed, "You don't know how to pray? Oh, come on."

"I don't." His blue eyes were sincere. "Brad, how do you pray?"

"Aw, you know how," I said. David's silence assured me that he didn't. I stopped and looked right at him. He really didn't know how to pray. I just couldn't imagine someone nine years old not knowing how to pray. Uneasy at my silence, David spoke again. "I think I know a little, but not the real way. Not the way they pray at Primary."

"Well, David, it's easy." Inside my mind I was quickly recalling all our family night lessons, all our family prayers, every blessing on the food. I couldn't understand why or how he had missed out on all this. "It's like this. . . ." David dropped his stick and listened intently.

"You open a formal prayer by addressing Heavenly Father." I had heard the steps so often, I recited them like a jumprope jingle. "Like in a letter, you say, 'Dear Heavenly Father,' then thank him for everything, then ask his blessing for everybody, then close 'In the name of Jesus Christ.' That's it." In my innocent fourth-grade mind I felt I had covered it all.

"Can I try it?" David promptly knelt down on a carpet of soft leaves (we always knelt in our Primary class). I got down next to him. He grinned, lowered his head and began.

I have always been taught to close my eyes during prayer, but that day my eyes were open. I wanted to see David as he offered his first prayer. With a little awkward prompting from me he got through it all right. When he was finished neither of us moved until David picked up his stick and asked, "Did I do okay?"

"Sure," I nodded, still kneeling in the yellow leaves. "That was great."

"Just four things to remember. Wow! Now I can pray any time."

As I look back on it now I did tell David the basic four parts that I had memorized for Primary and Sunday School, but I forgot to tell him one more thing. Of course, I really didn't know it in fourth grade, but some time between that walk home from Primary and now I learned the necessity to listen as well as to talk.

So often it's "Amen" and away. I need to give Heavenly Father a chance to respond so that our conversation will not be one-sided. If, after I pray, I spend some time listening, Heavenly Father might have an easier time getting through to me. Elder L. Tom Perry says, "It has been my personal experience if we will work things out in our minds, ask in faith, and be prepared to accept the direction we receive, the Lord will not deny us answers to prayers."

"Lord, what shall I do?" The words seem to come so easily when I'm struggling with a problem or have a difficult decision ahead. I need to remember that the decision is up to me. I must make it logically and intelligently, then ask God if my choice is correct.

God has promised answers
Every time I pray,
Sometimes in a minute,
Sometimes in a day.
It might take a decade
Till I plainly see
I've received the answer
God has promised me.

God has promised answers
Coming in all forms,
Sunlight on my mountains,
Snowflakes during storms,
Just a nice warm feeling
When I do my part;
Listening in faith brings
Answers to my heart.

The nice warm feeling I speak about in my poem is what the Lord has promised in Doctrine and Covenants 9:8, "And if it is right I will cause that your bosom shall burn within you."

It's always been comforting to know that Heavenly

Father will help me as I make important decisions; that he is always there and always listening.

As I visited the Sacred Grove on a trip through New York, I stood in awe among the verdant foliage as the afternoon sun slanted into the silence. I offered my reverent prayer of gratitude, thanking Heavenly Father for answering Joseph Smith's humble prayer in that same grove and for the testimony that incident has given me.

On that same trip, while spending a day in New York City, I met Jack Haring, Articles Editor of *Guideposts* Magazine. He has also edited *Boy's Life*, and *Exploring* for the Boy Scouts of America. While we talked over lunch he remembered back to when he was eighteen, "a teenage private," he related, "right in the middle of some of the fiercest fighting of World War II, the Battle of the Bulge, the final desperate attempt of the Germans to break through Allied lines in Belgium and dash to Antwerp and the sea."

He told me that he had just finished sleeping in the hayloft of a farmer's barn, that he hadn't had a hot meal for more than a week, when his squad leader, Sergeant Presto, shouted, "Collect your gear and fall out. We're going on a mission!"

It was apparent to Mr. Haring that I was totally enthralled, so he continued telling his story, which had recently appeared for the first time in *Guideposts*:

"We drove for about ten miles and then the trucks dropped us and sped away. It was dusk. Troops were strung out all along a dirt road that circled through some hills. When Presto came back from meeting with the platoon leader, he gathered the ten of us — we were one man short in the squad — around him.

" 'Okay, men, here's what we're going to do. This won't take long and we're going to travel light. Leave your packs and entrenching tools here.' He made it sound so simple. Intelligence had said that some German infantry were dug into a nearby hill and were causing havoc by shooting down on the roads in the area. Our battalion's job was to go up and flush them out.

"Single file on each side of the winding road, we moved up the hill. We moved quietly, warily. At the top, we were surprised to find, not Germans, but an abandoned chateau in the middle of a clearing. Our squad went into the building. . . .

" . . .Then Presto came stalking in. The Germans, he said, were in the woods beyond the clearing. Our orders were to chase them out into the waiting arms of another battalion positioned at the other end of the woods.

" 'There'll be three companies in this deal,' Presto said. 'Two of us will stretch out along the edge of the forest while the other hangs back in reserve. Now, as soon as we push into the woods, everybody fires, got it?'

"We spread out, walked through the darkness to the forest's edge, then, at a signal, we burst in, opening up with everything we had. We kept up a brisk pace, keeping contact with our buddies along the moving line, walking and firing for about a mile. But the forest was empty. There was no movement. . . .

"The trees in front of us exploded. Suddenly, the night went bright with every kind of firing I'd ever seen or heard of — rifles, rifle-launched grenades, mortars, machine guns, tracers over our heads, bullets at our thighs. But worst of all, Tiger tanks. At least six of them, opening up point-blank with 88-millimeter cannons. Their projectiles whined and crashed all up and down our line.

"*Our intelligence was wrong*, I thought angrily, as I flung myself down on my stomach. *They told us there were no tanks up here. Now we're really in for it.*

"Within seconds men were screaming in pain all around me. I saw a tree with a big trunk and made a sudden lunge to get behind it, but I wasn't quick enough. Something tore into my thigh. There was hot, searing pain.

"We were completely pinned down. The Tiger tanks kept scanning their turrets and firing on every yard of our line. The German ground troops sent their small arms fire into anything that moved.

"The minutes went by. Five. Ten. Fifteen. Then came a lull in the barrage. I called over to my best buddy, Kane. We called him 'Killer.' He was the gentlest guy in our platoon, but we'd nicknamed him that after the popular comic strip character, 'Killer Kane.'

" 'Are you hurt, Killer!'

" 'Naw. But I think everybody else over here is. Presto's hit bad.'

"I called to Cruz on my right. He was our squad's B.A.R. man. There was no answer. Then I barely heard him whispering, 'I'm hurt. Real bad. Floyd's dead. Corporal John's hit bad.'

"*Well,* I thought, *if Presto's out and the Corporal, too, we don't have a leader.*

"The pounding started again, this time with flares so they could spot us better. We did some firing back and then the action subsided into another lull.

"Down along the rear of our line came a figure, crawling. It was our platoon runner. 'Captain says we're getting nowhere,' he whispered to Killer and me. 'We're pulling back in five minutes. Move out when you hear our covering fire.'

"I crawled over to Killer. 'We've got to get our guys out of here,' I said. 'You go up your side and I'll go down mine, and we'll drag as many as possible to that big tree back there.'

" 'How're we going to get them out of here, though?'

" 'I don't know,' I said. 'But we can't leave them lying here.'

"We were trapped. I lay there on the cold ground feeling helpless, that forsaken feeling. Where was the God that I had prayed to during all those years of church and Sunday school back home in Pennsylvania? 'And whatsoever ye shall ask in My name, that will I do,' the Bible had said to me clearly. Was it necessary, when I needed help so badly, to ask?

" 'Oh, Lord,' I mumbled, 'help us. We're trying to get our wounded buddies out of here. Show us the way.'

"I had no sooner started dragging Corporal John toward our meeting tree when the firing started up in the center of our line. *There's the signal for pulling back,* I thought frantically, *but we can't do it. The Germans will sweep in on us; they'll mop us up before we can pull back.*

"Just as I got to the tree, I saw that Killer had brought back three wounded squad members. So we had six in all to get back. I closed my eyes and in desperation said, 'In Your name, Lord, help us.'

"I opened my eyes. In the black of night, moving mysteriously among the shattered trees, a giant hulk came toward us. *The Germans,* my heart thumped, *they've broken out of the brush. They're bearing down on us.* No, it was something else, something unbelievable. It now came into full view and stopped beside our tree.

"A horse.

"A big, docile, shaggy chestnut, standing there without a harness, as though awaiting our bidding.

"Killer and I looked at each other in disbelief. We didn't question then where the horse came from, or how, or why; we just got to work. Moving swiftly, we draped Cruz and the Corporal on the chestnut's broad back, then Mike and Presto. Then, with Killer carrying one of our buddies and me carrying the other, we led the horse out of the woods. At the clearing the horse trotted on ahead of us, straight to the chateau, and by the time Killer and I got there, our wounded were already on medical stretchers. The two men we carried in were cared for; the medics gave a quick look at my shrapnel wound; and then, as fast as we could, Killer and I went to find the horse. We wanted to pat him, give him some sugar, anything to make him sense our gratitude.

"But he wasn't there. We looked everywhere, asked everyone we saw, but no one could tell us anything about him. He had simply vanished — gone from us as mysteriously as he had come. . . ."

Heavenly Father answered Jack Haring's prayer and he will answer mine. So I'll continue to pray — alone, with family, with friends. I'll also try to be honest and pray sincerely, for only genuine prayers reach heaven.

Thanks to Mr. Jones, my high school drama teacher, I've learned to love Shakespeare. The eternal truths that he has left the world in his works have helped me over many rough times. His thought from Hamlet about prayer really pierced me. The first time I ever read it I was so impressed that I lettered it on a large piece of paper and put it up in my room:

> My words fly up, my thoughts remain below.
> Words without thoughts never to heaven go.

For me, this is the hardest challenge — to pray sincerely. I know that whether I'm standing at a pulpit, kneeling by my bed, or driving on a busy freeway my prayer will be heard if it is from my heart. And if I know that, why do I continue to occasionally pray with just words?

During my junior year in high school we were reading *The Adventures of Huckleberry Finn*, by Mark Twain. It was Thursday night. I knew there was a test Friday so I brushed my teeth, kissed Mom and Dad goodnight, grabbed my book and took off to my bedroom. I was almost twenty-five pages behind in assigned reading. I had to catch up, and catch up that night! I knelt down hurriedly by the side of my bed and whipped off some absurd, insincere thing that I was willing to let pass as a prayer. Then, climbing into bed and opening my book, I began reading the words the author put into the mouth of Huck Finn:

"I about made up my mind to pray, and see if I couldn't try to quit being the kind of boy I was and be better. So I kneeled down. But the words wouldn't come. Why wouldn't they? It warn't no use to try and hide it from Him. . . . I knowed very well why they wouldn't come. It was because my heart warn't right; it was because . . . I was holding on to the biggest [sin] of all. I was tryin' to make my mouth *say* I would do the right thing and the clean thing . . . but deep down in me I knowed it was a lie, and He knowed it. You can't pray a lie — I found that out."

Needless to say, I dropped back down on my knees and asked forgiveness for my insincerity. Now, when it is late and I am tired, when I kneel down offering a prayer with just words and no real feeling, I climb between the sheets and remember Huck Finn and the lesson we both had to recognize, that an insincere prayer is worthless. "You can't pray a lie."

Bishop H. Burke Peterson said, "Sincere prayer is the heart of a happy and productive life."

So, for me, praying is step one, the first and continuing step to be taken as I climb my mountain to perfection. In other words, as I *try*!

3

What's Best For Me Now?

"You need to do what?" The counselor's huge smile faded to a blank, open-mouthed stare.

I halfway cleared my throat. "I need to drop 8½ credits," I repeated.

Uncomfortably she leaned back in her chair.

"I know it's only my second week of college." I sat forward. "And I know I just started at BYU, but —."

"Young man," she smiled all-knowingly, "I'm afraid what you're asking is completely out of the question."

"I don't think you understand," I began again.

"No, young man, I don't think *you* understand." She strained forward and tapped her desk officiously. "You're a beginning freshman, am I right?"

I nodded.

"All new students have a hard adjustment period. You can't just give up the first moment the going gets rough."

"No, Mrs. — "

"Finney," she stated.

"Well, that's not it, Mrs. Finney. I like BYU, and I like the classes I have. There's just something else I have to do before my mission."

She raised her eyebrows condescendingly. "Now what do you have to do that's more important than an education?"

I swallowed. "I have to finish my book."

She tried to disguise her surprise, but her face looked as if someone had just used her to demonstrate the Heimlich maneuver. "How old did you say you are?"

"Eighteen." I deepened my voice. "Almost nineteen."

"And you are writing a book?"

I nodded.

"Well, young man, as much as I'd like to help you I'm afraid it's impossible."

This interview was becoming frustrating. "Mrs. Finney, I have to be able to finish this book before my mission. Since school began I haven't been — "

"Young man," she interrupted, "there is no need to talk so fast." She gave me a let-me-relate-to-you look. "I'm not going anywhere, so please begin again."

"As I said, I haven't been able to do any good writing for two weeks. I spend all day on campus and all night doing homework."

"And I don't suppose you could write this little book on weekends?"

Resisting the urge to explode, I tightened my grip on some books in my lap. "No, Mrs. Finney." I was deliberately keeping my voice in control. "Maybe someone else could finish a book and still keep up in school, but I can't. I'm a slow writer. I always have been."

"How do you expect me to tell your parents?" she asked, as though I'd just been caught shoplifting.

"I've already talked to them about it," I said. "I've even prayed." Inside I wondered at which other university but BYU I could have said that and been understood.

"It's just come down to deciding what's best for me, and right now that means dropping half my classes."

"You know, ah —"

"Brad," I supplied.

"Yes, Brad, I have freshmen in this office all the time wanting to drop their P.E. credit, or science classes." I shifted nervously. "By now I've heard every excuse ever invented. But a book! I must give you credit for originality."

Why wouldn't she listen to me? "Mrs. Finney," I sighed, "I still don't think you understand."

"Oh, but I do. You've made a decision and you feel good about it."

"Exactly!" I exclaimed. "And I'm afraid right now my education is standing in the way of my education. Do you know what I mean?"

She nodded dubiously.

"That's why I've decided to drop these hours."

"But you can't." The counselor leaned back once more in her heavy chair.

My entire insides dropped a foot as she continued. "You see, Brad, to keep your scholarship you need at least 15 credit hours. Drop 8½ and I'm afraid you'll be dropping. . . ."

"The scholarship?"

"Precisely." She said the word almost triumphantly.

My scholarship! In all my deciding and figuring, why hadn't I thought of that? I felt a tightness bind me; a sick tenseness such as I always get before a penicillin shot. "All right," I determined realistically. "Something has to go, and it has to go now." Every half-finished chapter waiting on my bedroom desk, the full tuition scholarship, and my almost-zero savings account all flashed wildly across my mind. I asked under my breath, "What is best for me now?"

Mrs. Finney picked up her pen and tapped it rhythmically on her desk. "I think you should keep the eighteen hours you have and forget this idea of writing a book. After all, scholarships don't come that easily."

She sounded a bit irritated at having spent so long with me. I stood awkwardly but didn't respond.

It sounds such an easy thing to decide what's important. Is it good? Is it bad? right? wrong? building or hurting? As opportunities come, usually the decision is simple. But now and then I find that step two, making a value judgment — deciding what is important enough for me to try for — is almost the hardest trying step of all. While I stood there silently, Mrs. Finney neatened her tidy desk.

"Brad," she said, looking intently at the wall clock, "make up your mind; or I could see you at 1:30 after my lunch." She stood up and indicated the door.

I arranged my books in my arms and started out. "I hope," she said seriously, "that you'll realize your scholarship is more important than your whim. There are hundreds of students out there who would give a lot for what you are thinking of giving up."

I smiled because I didn't know what else to do. As much as I wanted to, I knew I couldn't keep both. I had tried for two weeks, and it hadn't worked at all. That's why I decided to drop classes and finish the book in the first place. But my scholarship? Could I give that up? I knew she thought me stupid to consider it.

Leaving the Administration Building, I headed toward the library. Why couldn't I just slip peacefully away into a Rip Van Winkle sleep and wake up in three months with the book completed and passing grades in every class? I settled myself at a vacant table on the second floor.

Here I was again, right back where I had started two weeks earlier. I had already decided what was best for me, and now this scholarship thing had messed it all up. "What should I do?" I asked myself again.

As I sat there in the library I recalled a comment I once heard that virtually every good principle was displayed by the young Nephi. I asked myself, What value judgment had he made, for example?

Well, he willingly followed the leadership of his prophet father by leaving the comforts of Jerusalem for a hard life in the rugged wilderness. He placed more importance on doing the Lord's will than on physical comfort or even on what his peers might say about his decision. And having made that value judgment he stayed with it. He never complained or looked back.

His older brothers Laman and Lemuel were quite a different case. Faced with the same decision, they were unwilling to leave their home comforts, and in the wilderness they constantly grouched and grumbled and harked back to the "good times" and the easier life they had left behind. You wonder sometimes why they didn't just leave the group and return to live at Jerusalem. By their attitude you would suppose they really had made their value judgment — Jerusalem and its attractions were for them! Yet they didn't make a clear-cut decision either to go back or to go on, otherwise why didn't they act on that judgment and feel good about it?

Feel good about it. That was the key. Nephi prayed and received a firm answer which directed him to the more difficult course of action — an action which, humanly speaking, probably looked rather silly. But he was happy to do it. He made a value judgment; he had to live with that judgment for the rest of his life; and he felt good about it.

In a milder way, wasn't that my case? I glanced at the wall clock in the library. One-fifteen. I said a silent prayer, adding it to those I had previously offered on this subject. Now I had to make *my* value judgment. I had to live with it. And I had to feel good about it.

Because you are reading this book, you know the choice I made.

Of course, as my sister-in-law, Margo, reminds me, "Making value judgments is only half of this free-agency thing." She's right. For me, it's always been just as hard to accept a value judgment as it has been to make one. And that thought takes me back to the mission decision.

I didn't share the driver's cheerfulness that afternoon as he yelled "Everybody out!" and our yellow school bus jerked to a stop. I stood from my window seat and started slowly to the front of the nearly empty bus. The metal doors unfolded. I shivered as the late fall breeze forced its way under my light jacket. As the bus chugged away I wedged my ninth-grade book *New Horizons in Literature* between my knees and zipped the jacket. The lower half of the bus vanished over the hill. I would have been on the bus clear to Columbia Lane, where my bus stop used to be, if it hadn't been for Sister Milhouse. That very morning she had scolded the bus driver and complained, "All those rowdy children are bothering my dog." Now, thanks to her, I had to walk five extra blocks to get home. I kicked a lopsided rock onto the road in front of me and began the trek.

I wanted to turn off my brain, but when I got to the four-way stop I was thinking so much about not thinking that I gave up and decided to think again anyway. I thought about my new bus stop, Sister Milhouse, and the chilling five-extra-block walk I would be facing all winter.

Just to break the monotony I picked up the rock I'd been kicking and tossed it ahead. It must have aroused that funny little dog. "Yip, yip, yip!" The high-pitched yelps were piercing.

"Yip, yip," I mimicked, as I stooped over and made a face through the fence.

Four stubby legs straightened and the dog leaped up and down as though it were on a trampoline. It yelped and snarled even as I walked away. That tiny, obnoxious dog was trying to scare me. I had to laugh at the thought. The animal was only one handspan high and was so old he couldn't see. Sister Milhouse came plowing out of her front door.

"Get away! Get away from that fence!"

"I was just —"

"I know what you were doing," she bellowed. "Get away and leave my little Prissy alone."

Prissy, the fat mass of tangled fur, waddled and limped toward her mistress. Lindsay Adams said the reason Prissy walked strangely was that a Christmas tree fell on her once.

Sister Milhouse's eyes flashed. "I won't have you tormenting this innocent creature."

"But I didn't do anything!" I shouted over the dog's yelps.

"Don't you Wilcox boys have any respect?"

That was it! I'd had about all I could take. Deliberately I pitched a rock at her chain link fence and walked away. Behind me Prissy flipped into total hysteria as the metal fence vibrated.

"That's a fine way for a future missionary to act," Sister Milhouse hollered.

I whipped around and stared back at her. Knowing Sister Milhouse, I knew what would hurt her most. "I'm not going on a mission anyway, so there!"

As I look back on it, I know I just wanted to shock her. But I had said the words, and in my worldly-wise fifteen-year-old way I felt I had made a value judgment I would have to live by. I wasn't going on a mission, and that was that.

At our house I stormed through the back door and into my bedroom. "I'm not going," I huffed. "Mission, mission, mission — I'm sick of it. Just because my brothers go, everybody thinks I'm going." I flopped down on my bed right under the I-Will-Follow-The-Prophet poster that had been taped to my wall since I was eight. With both hands I threw my English book against the dresser. "It's not right to say 'Every young man serve a mission.' I'm not going to throw away two whole years of my life."

That night I hardly slept. I kept telling myself, "You're happy. It feels good to give up memorizing scriptures and saving money." Then, secretly I wondered why I felt so miserable.

I dragged through the next few days of school, always making sure to walk across the street in the weeds whenever I passed Sister Milhouse's. I didn't want to face her or that ugly Prissy.

"When I do good, I feel good. When I do not do good I do not feel good." I reread the quotation by Abraham Lincoln which was lettered in the school library. If that's true, then why did I feel rotten when I was doing good? I had made my value judgment — a mission was not for me. Then why didn't I feel happy?

Now, looking back on it, I see that what I didn't realize then was that this value judgment had already been made by Heavenly Father. Whether I chose to accept that judgment and go on a mission or reject it and stay does not alter the fact that a mission is best. The prophet said "*every* young man," not "everyone except Brad Wilcox."

Dropping 8½ credits and giving up a scholarship is a matter of making a value judgment. This mission decision was a matter of accepting one already made.

Finally, when I couldn't stand feeling miserable anymore, I decided that if Heavenly Father felt that a mission is so important that he would command me to go, then I had better adjust my thinking fast and find out why. I wanted to follow the prophet, but I would not follow blindly.

It took months of figuring things out within myself to regain my eternal perspective. I prayed until I finally felt worthy to take the I-Will-Follow-The-Prophet sign out of the closet and tape it back above my bed where it belonged. The room had seemed empty and out of focus. Now, with my sign back up, I felt focused again, too. It was terrific to be able to promise Heavenly Father that I would serve an honorable mission. When I do so it will be because serving God and my fellowman on a mission is the best thing for me, and not because it's best for my Mom and Dad, or a girl friend — or even Sister Milhouse.

Through scriptures and prophets God has told us that certain things are important to do or not do in this life. Some things are good for us. Some things are not. The value judgments have been made. It now becomes my responsibility to accept those value judgments and, more importantly, to know why. Why prepare for that temple marriage? Why pay tithing? Why participate in family home evening and go to church meetings? Why try? My friend, Martha Nibley, summed it up well in a seminary devotional once: "We must avoid sin as a result of intelligent decision rather than ignorant fear."

But what if Heavenly Father is wrong? What if the value judgments he has made are not really best for me? I know this is ridiculous and I can hardly believe I wrote it, but look around and count the people who believe it's true. I think of the times in my own life when I wondered if God had my best interests in mind.

When Mr. Webb's biology final rolled around and I hadn't done any study to speak of, it was easy for me to rationalize: "Surely Heavenly Father wants me to pass the test. I know I haven't studied enough and have missed some classes and have no right to do well, but I also know God wants what's best for me. And right now, to have what's best means I must cheat." I managed to convince myself in effect that Heavenly Father's value judgment about honesty was great for everyone else, but was not for me. Surprise! I was wrong again.

Now I'd like to introduce you to a remarkable man, my great-grandfather Harry Hale Russell. Though I never met him I have come to know him well through the A-number-one best grandma in the world, Mary Russell Camenish. Unlike a lot of my friends whose grandparents live entire continents away, I've been able to grow up with Grandma right down the street. She was the only girl Dad let me date before I was sixteen, and she has remained my steady girl friend ever since.

One day while I was at her house for something (I rarely remember exactly what I go for except to have her offer me root beer and M and M candies), I heard her upstairs.

"Grandma?" I called.

"I'm up here."

I headed up the winding staircase toward what once was my mom's room. It is a blue room with a large four-poster bed central to the inside wall. Because of the slanted ceiling and gabled windows, I always felt as if I were at Disneyland or in some old movie.

"Hello, Brad." I gave Grandma a hug. She was sorting through some built-in drawers.

"It's taken me forever, but I'm finally getting this old stuff sorted and put away."

I began shuffling through some aged photographs lying on the quilt-covered bed. I pulled a picture out of the pile. "Grandma, isn't this your father?"

She pushed the last drawer into the wall. "Yes, that's your great-grandfather about the time he was baptized."

"He looks strong." I stared at the handsome man in the antique frame.

"He was strong," Grandma laughed. "Strong-willed, anyway. Mama wondered if he'd ever join the Church." Grandma took the picture and held it fondly.

"You know, Brad, he was an intelligent man. In fact, it was his intellectual pride that finally trapped him into studying his wife's religion." She cleared a place on the bed and sat down next to me.

"When Oscar, my oldest brother, announced he wished to be baptized on his eighth birthday, Papa was first amused, then angry. He firmly refused his consent. Mama had taught us the gospel, and that night as we knelt for prayers she told my disappointed brother, 'If we pray in faith, the Lord will soften your father's heart and he'll consent to your baptism.' "

Grandma spoke right to me. "I'm amazed that Mama ever said such a thing, to be honest with you. For we all knew how stubborn Papa was in religious matters. The next day he came home in the middle of the morning. Mama asked again if Oscar could be baptized. And Papa said abruptly, 'I thought baptism was for the remission of sins. That boy's never committed any sin.' Mama knew better than to argue, but she faced him steadily. 'He's eight years old. That's when he's supposed to be baptized.' We all stared at her and then at Papa. 'All right!' he said finally. 'Let him be baptized.' "

"Yes," Grandma recalled, "I think that baptism is what finally did it. That's when Papa decided to study the Church and prove to everyone that it was false. Sure enough," Grandma smiled again at the picture in her hand, "he studied to disprove it and proved himself right into it. On July the seventh, 1912, Papa was baptized and confirmed, and his conversion to the gospel was total. As he always said, 'I swallowed the bait, hook, line and pole.' "

"That's the way he lived, Brad. When Papa believed something was right, I mean when he knew that something was best for him, he was uncompromising. Like tithing." Grandma patted my hand. "When Papa became a member of the Church he scrupulously added up all his assets and figured he owed the Lord $3,500 in tithing.

"Even today that's a huge sum of money; but in 1912, to a man with seven children to support, the acquisition of so much cash money seemed impossible, until a man walked into our house one night and announced that he felt impelled to pay Papa an almost forgotten debt amounting to $2,700. So Papa paid his tithing in full."

Grandma stood and we started downstairs. "He had always been a heavy smoker, too. In fact, he had smoked continually for twenty years. That was back in the days when all the men carried their sacks of tobacco and rolled cigarettes themselves. Well, the day before his baptism, to Mama's great concern, Papa was still smoking. 'Don't worry,' he declared. 'I'm giving it all up tomorrow. Today I'll smoke all I want.'

"By that afternoon," Grandma admitted, "we all had to leave the house because there was so much smoke." She stopped to remember. "Yes, I think there was a cigarette in his mouth all day long. But when our old clock bonged midnight, that was the end. He said he'd never use tobacco again and he never did. Papa hated hypocrisy."

I followed Grandma into the kitchen. "How could it have been so easy for him to quit if he'd smoked for twenty years?" I asked.

"Oh, it wasn't easy," Grandma laughed, and offered me some M and M's at last. "He always kept one small sack of tobacco on his dresser. I remember Papa would stare at that sack and ask himself, 'Which is bigger, you or me?' "

Grandma bustled about preparing a glass of root beer for me. "No, it wasn't easy for him to quit smoking, but he lived the Word of Wisdom because he knew it was best for him and for his family. If it hadn't been, nothing on earth could have made Papa give up that habit."

Later in his life, Harry Hale Russell went on to invent the Temple Index Bureau system, which largely eliminated duplication in temple work for the dead. "It was an inspired invention that took years of struggle and sacrifice, but he never gave up because it was the right thing." That's what Grandma told me.

Sitting in her sun-warmed kitchen I thought about the next life when my great-grandfather and I will meet. I will be proud to tell him how much I admire him for accepting the value judgments that Heavenly Father has made.

Grandma sat across from me at the table. Through the window behind her sunlight hazily diffused her image. "Yes," she said, "when Papa knew something was best for him he was uncompromising."

Thanks to Janath Russell Cannon for the information about Harry Hale Russell in her unpublished article, "There Is a Destiny."

4

That's What You Get—Nothing

The colored Christmas lights blinked on and off and on and off, winking at me through the fogged department store window. Shoppers hurried along the icy sidewalk balancing armfuls of packages in the biting wind. But we were in no hurry that day. We just walked slowly from window to window, laughing at the mechanical figures and Christmas toy displays.

My friend (whom I will call Tim) and I both had last-minute shopping to do. So when he had called that morning I had been more than willing to volunteer a car and an afternoon to spend downtown.

"Dad, may I take the car about one o'clock?" I asked.

"Have you finished clearing the table?" Dad called from the living room, where he was still fussing over a faulty bulb on our tree lights.

I scowled at the breakfast dishes I was supposed to have cleared away three hours ago, and was just beginning to answer that question when another came flying in low from the living room.

"Is the family room straightened up yet? Didn't Mom ask you to do the bathrooms, too?" Dad's voice sounded like a broken record as he repeated the questions I had heard earlier. He came walking around the corner with some empty ornament boxes he was carrying downstairs. "And how about that pile of dirty clothes in your bedroom?"

"Dad," I interrupted, "I just need to take the car at one o'clock, okay?"

"If your chores are finished, it's fine."

"Come on," I moaned, as though I had just been asked to hike to Mars. "How do you expect me to do all that by one o'clock?"

"Well, son, it's up to you. If you really need that car you'll find a way." Even though he was halfway downstairs, I could tell that Dad was wearing his I-won't-bend-on-this-one look. "After all," he went on, "you've known what you've needed to do ever since breakfast."

"Yeah, but —"

"No buts, Brad." Dad's voice was a muffled boom from the cement walls of the storage room. "If you want to use the family car. . . ."

He didn't have to finish. I had heard this broken record before, too. To use the family car, I had to do my share of the family work. Mumbling to myself I turned and headed for my bedroom to attack the week-old pile of soiled shirts, dirty socks, and stiff jeans.

It was about 1:30 when Tim and I pulled into the small parking lot behind J.C. Penney's. As I locked the door and pocketed the key I had to admit Dad was right. My chores were all done because I wanted the car, and now I had it until six o'clock.

"Hey, Brad, look at that one." Tim laughed and pointed into the store window. "I wonder how they got it clear up there?"

I leaned closer to the glass for a better look. "Now, that really looks great! Realistic, you know what I mean?" I stood up straight again and buried my bare fingers in the tight pockets of my old jeans.

"Too bad it's so expensive. I just never have enough money," I complained. I stood gazing into that miniature world of Santa Claus robots, treasure chests, electronic basketball and eight-track tapes. Someone had filled that window with more magical Christmas surprises than I ever imagined. "Tim, you know Aaron, my cousin? Well, I got his name in the family gift exchange and I know he'd love that. . . ."

I turned and realized Tim wasn't by my side. "Tim?" I called. "Where'd you go?"

From up ahead he yelled over his shoulder, "Brad, come here, quick!"

Tim was crouched against the red brick wall of the next building. "Look at this. Look at what I just found."

I knelt down next to him.

"Brad, there's money in here." The wallet in his hand was open and Tim kept running his thumb over the green bills. It was a small leather wallet and, judging from the flowery workmanship, a woman's.

"See if there's any identification."

Tim hurriedly poked between all the flaps. "Here's something." He pulled out a white card. It was an I.D. card all right, the kind that comes in all new wallets, only it had never been filled out.

"Wait," Tim said. From between the bills he pulled a folded note and opened it.

"Remember to call Alan Bullock," he read.

"That's a big help," I snorted. "Who in the world is Alan Bullock?"

"I don't know," Tim replied, folding the wallet closed again. "But I'm going to find out. I'll look him up in the phone book and call him. Isn't there a pay phone in the next block? He'll know who owns the wallet, then we'll look them up, drive over there, give them the money, and the. . . ."

We both stood up.

As if he were in a trance, Tim continued, ". . .and the lady will be in tears, and she'll come running to the door, and she'll put an article in the paper about me, and maybe you, too. I'll bet she even gives me fifty dollars at least, for being so honest."

"All right," I said. "But when you find out who this woman is you'd better find out if she lives nearby, because the gas is almost on empty."

Tim shoved the wallet in his front pocket and started around the corner to the pay phone. "I'll meet you in the parking lot in about fifteen minutes," he yelled.

Here we were, right in the middle of the plot of some old

Hardy Boys' mystery. All the way back down the street I found myself eyeing the sidewalk. "There must have been two hundred dollars in that wallet," I thought. "Two hundred dollars at Christmastime! Maybe there is an unidentified wallet waiting for me, too. Whoever did own that wallet is lucky we found it." I turned the corner past the department store window with the blinking lights and walked on toward the parking lot. My thoughts ran on. "If this were a Sunday School lesson, I guess Tim would be the good, selfless example. He sure is going the extra mile. He really is doing the right thing."

As I crunched through the icy alley to our meeting place I was surprised to find Tim already there. It had only taken me about five minutes to get back to the car.

"Hurry, Brad," he called. "I know who lost the wallet."

We climbed into the old car and chugged out into the street.

"Head down to the lake," Tim directed. "That Bullock guy knew exactly who lost it because she'd called him last night. How much do you think she'll give us?"

"For what?" I asked.

"For bringing her wallet back."

"Oh, I don't know. Sometimes you read about where people give half, and sometimes nothing. It all depends."

Finally, we found the house by the lake. I parked in the driveway.

"Aren't you coming?" Tim asked excitedly.

"No, I'll just wait here."

"You've gotta come, Brad. You deserve the reward, too."

I shoved my door open and joined Tim on the front porch. He grinned confidently at me, rang the doorbell, and stepped back. Almost immediately a young woman answered.

"Hello," she said, stroking a stray strand of hair away from her face. "You must be the young men who found my money. Alan just called." She opened the screen door and Tim handed her the wallet.

"We won't come in, Ma'am, our shoes are kinda wet. I just wanted to bring your wallet back."

She checked inside and looked relieved. "Thank you, ah. . . ."

"Tim. My name is Tim. This is Brad." I nodded.

"You'll never know what this means." The woman held the wallet close. "With Christmas round the corner, and all."

"I sure do," Tim replied. "I don't have any Christmas money this year."

Looking away to hide my embarrassed smile, I thought, "That's pretty pointed, Tim." That's when I saw the two little girls, with dark eyes like their mother's, peeking and flirting from behind the door.

"Well, thank you." The woman smiled and began to close the door.

"Ma'am." Tim cleared his throat. "There's no identification in that wallet. You should fill out that card in there."

"I know," she said lightly. "I just bought the silly thing and haven't even put my driver's license in it yet."

"Well, I'm sure glad we took the trouble to find out."

"So am I," she smiled.

"Yep, I'm really glad I found you okay and brought back all that money."

"I know you didn't have to go to all this extra trouble," the woman said quietly.

Tim gave me a here-it-comes nudge.

"You are an extremely honest young man. You've just done something I'll always remember." Gathering the children back into the room, she shut the door.

Tim stood stunned. I knew what he was thinking. I could almost hear the thud of his hopes hitting the ground.

"It's her money," I reasoned aloud.

Tim stared at the door. "But if I hadn't. . . ."

"You don't have to tell me."

The wind was cold. Snow had begun to fall, and there was already a light blanket across my windshield. Tim slammed the car door. "That'll teach me! Do a good turn and whadaya get? Nuthin! Not a darn thing! 'Thank you,' " he mimicked insipidly.

We drove in silence for a time until Tim started up again. "All that work for nuthin!" He leaned forward, switched on the radio and tuned it from station to station. I didn't know if I should speak or not, but I did.

"Nothing? You gave that lady back her money, didn't you?"

"Yeah, and it took all afternoon, too. A whole afternoon," he repeated, "shot down the tubes. She owed me a reward and didn't even give me back my dime for the phone call. Talk about ungrateful! Where's her Christmas spirit?"

I reminded, "She did say thanks."

"Thanks," Tim laughed. "What a joke! Anyone else would have just taken the dumb money. But me! I have to be Mr. Honest-seminary-president-hero type. Nobody will ever even know I did this."

He slumped down in the seat and didn't talk again until I dropped him off. My whole afternoon was gone, along with whatever Christmas spirit I had had earlier. I steered the car into Tim's driveway.

"I just don't get it, Brad. I thought you were supposed to feel good when you do unto others, and all that stuff."

"Yeah," I said, shifting into neutral so I could take my foot off the clutch. "I guess it shouldn't matter that you didn't get any reward from her. I mean, she did say how much she needed it right now, but. . . ."

Tim pulled his scarf tight around his neck. "Nuthin!" He opened his door. "That's what you get for doing the right thing, nuthin!" He climbed out of the car. The chill wind flooded through the open door. "See ya, Brad. Merry Christmas, and all that stuff."

I waved and shifted into reverse. The old tires slid a little on the fresh snow, but the roads were still clear. On the trip home the radio might as well have been turned off. My mind was muddled with thoughts of a wasted afternoon and the present I didn't get to buy for Aaron. When I finally started up our long driveway it was just beginning to get dark. Everything seemed to melt together into a blue-gray December evening.

I loved the sight of our house surrounded warmly by trees. White snow on red brick seemed an appropriate Christmas contrast. Dad's masterpiece, the Christmas tree, which he fiddled to finality after the rest of us had had our fill of decorating, glowed softly through our large living room window. Gently the blowing snow featherstitched a pattern on the chill air. I smiled at Mom's Christmas bells which traditionally hang on our front door every year. Having parked the car, I entered this Christmas-card scene, making sure I left only the most even and measured footprints in the newly fallen snow.

My "Bah, humbug!" attitude was almost forgotten along with my cold, gloveless fingers. Why had I felt so terrible for doing a good turn which was worthy of a feature story in the *New Era*? Suddenly it seemed laughable. I could just see Tim's face on the cover of the next issue.

"Oh, hi, Brad!" Chris, my younger brother, had barreled upstairs and almost over the top of me. He hoisted a broom and passed me at the back door. "I'm going to sweep the snow off the porch before it sticks."

"Glad to see you home." Dad looked over his adding machine on the kitchen counter.

"The car still goes, Dad," I reported. "No flat tires, but almost out of gas."

Just then Mom called her "welcome home" from the direction of the bedroom. It felt good to be home. "What a fantastic family!" I thought, sagely. "Everybody doing his part, working together — but what about me?" I shrugged and settled comfortably into the rug to read the evening paper, but again the thought flashed through my mind in total Christmas technicolor. "What about me? My chores, the breakfast dishes, the dirty clothes. Everyone working together except me. Sure, I did my chores, but not to do my share around the house, or to help Mom and Dad, or the hundred other good reasons I might have had. I did them because I wanted to use the car."

Ordinarily I could have ignored such feelings, but because it was Christmas I felt selfish and ashamed. I had done the right thing, but for the wrong reason. Then I remembered Tim's words: "That's what you get for doing the right thing, nuthin!"

It was clear to me now: That's what you get for having the wrong reasons! Triumphant with this newly discovered truth, I turned to Dad and explained: "Doing the right thing is supposed to bring happiness, and it does when you have the right reasons. But if you do right for the wrong reasons. . . . Oh, Dad, no wonder Tim felt so bad." Dad looked puzzled.

"All that work for nuthin! That's what we said. Both of us said it. But it wasn't for nothing at all!" I was talking so fast I could hardly listen to myself.

"Tim didn't get what he wanted when he did the right thing, so he was disappointed. I did get what I wanted, yet I was disappointed, too. But neither one of us should have been disappointed. We just needed the right reasons. *Doing the right thing for the right reasons*. That's the key, Dad," I declared enthusiastically. "That's the key."

Reasons, motives: it seems our whole lives revolve around them. Everything we try, right or wrong, we try for a reason. I liked what I had learned; it seemed to follow me through Christmas and flipped in and out of my mind during the next few months. So when Lisa, a twelve-year-old neighbor friend, was talking with me on my front porch in March, it seemed natural for me to take the role of all-knowing, all-wise senior-high-school guru.

Lisa's problem was that when she learned to sew, her only motivation was for Rob, the boy she wanted to impress, to notice her new homemade dress. Lisa had made the dress, but when she got to school she was let down because Rob hardly even noticed her, let alone her dress. "All that work for nothing," she said in a defeated tone.

"He didn't even look at me, and I made it myself, except where Mom helped a little, but I picked the colors. I heard him say his sister makes all her clothes, and. . . ."

I knew why Lisa felt so bad. She did the right thing for a good reason, but it wasn't reason enough. Getting Rob's attention was a single and rather weak motive for learning to sew. Besides, if this Rob was anything like I used to be in seventh grade, it would take a lot more than a new yellow dress to get him to actually look at a girl.

"It was all for nothing!" she wailed again, burying her head in her skirt.

"Lisa," I began, "let me tell you about something I call multi-motives."

Her red head popped up, but she looked at me as though I were speaking Swedish or something.

"It's like this. Whenever I do anything important —"

"Like learning to sew?" she asked.

"Exactly. I make myself have more than one reason. I am Lisa," I began teasing in foolish falsetto, "and I will learn to sew to save money, to serve others, to develop a lifelong skill, to —"

"To help my Mom." She laughed.

"And, because there is a boy at school I hope will notice me." She blushed as I continued, "because he is really good looking, but not quite as good looking as my best neighbor and only true boy friend, Brad." I glanced sideways to see why she wasn't laughing at what I thought was funny enough to gag a maggot. She just stared at me with wide eyes.

"All those are pretty good reasons," she said.

"Sure they are, Lisa. And now, when Rob doesn't pay any attention to the pretty things you sew, you don't have to care. All that work wasn't for nothing. It was for something. Look at all you've accomplished." I nudged her playfully.

"But if he does —" she began to smile.

"If he does notice, then that's just an extra good feeling."

Lisa stood up and started to say good-bye.

"You see, Lisa," I straightened the little handmade bow at her neck, "Rob noticing your dress needs to be the *result* of an action, and not the *cause*. Do you understand?"

"Sure I do," she giggled. "Thanks, Brad." I watched girl and dress disappear at the end of the driveway.

"Boy," I thought, "there goes one clear-thinking twelve-year-old. She understands a principle that took me years longer to see."

To me it seems some people never grasp this concept at all. For example:

Archibald, the guy who tries out for the football team and willingly gets wounded at every practice just because his girl friend loves football players. Old Archibald is going to be crushed when Minnehaha, or whatever her name is, trots off and leaves him holding a huge responsibility to his team, coach, and student body; a responsibility that he doesn't want and got only because of a single motive. Minnehaha gave him the incentive to try, and that's great; but Archibald wouldn't feel so bad right now if he'd had other motives as well. Multi-motives. He would feel better if he had decided, "I want to play football to develop my body and coordination, to support and represent my school, to make new friends, to learn sportsmanship, and besides, my girl friend loves football players." Then, when Minnehaha cuts out, Archibald can still feel fulfilled and content with his decision.

Mrs. Noteworthy, a prominent local civic leader donating funds and time in the hope of newspaper coverage or of winning a valuable-citizen award.

High school students' working, even cheating, for good grades to qualify for important scholarships or to satisfy their parents' pride.

My friend Tim, an honest young citizen returning a lost wallet, feeling justified in expecting a sizable reward.

Missionary, the eldest son of the family accepting a call to serve in order to meet his parents' expectations. "My folks always wanted me to go on a mission."

The list is endless. The prospect of money, fame, honor or attention are all motives which might spur me toward self-betterment, and that's good as long as I remember that these weak, single motives make trying a bigger risk than it needs to be.

While climbing my mountain to perfection, multi-motives can guard me from disappointment and depression when that scholarship doesn't come through, or when the girl I've been working to impress still says, "Who?" when I phone her for a date.

Too often I make the hike up my mountain harder than it needs to be.

At that time in my life, I was sure I knew everything about right reasons, wrong reasons, and multi-motives. But when it came time for the annual top scholar awards, in which the top speech and drama student in the state is selected, I realized I had bypassed the most important thing about them. It is difficult for me to write about it even now, but it was a lesson I needed to learn. I hope to remember it my whole life long.

The instant the telecast was over I started away from the

crowd. I don't remember how I manipulated my way through the crush of people, but somehow I managed to reach the stage door.

"Too bad," a woman said as I passed. "I guess everyone can't be the winner."

"Yeah," I smiled. Inside I was not smiling. I wanted to run, hit, scream. With total concentration, I simply walked slowly to the end of the hall and pushed open the heavy door; then broke into the run I needed so desperately. The halls were strange and foreign, but I ran up a flight of stairs, past a dimly lighted trophy case, and into another empty corridor.

"Too bad," I repeated bitterly to myself. Everyone can't be a winner. But I wasn't even named runner-up! I wasn't even named anything.

I fought back the anger. It wasn't fair. I was better qualified than anyone there. Where was honesty? Where was justice? Surely even the winners knew within themselves that the judges were wrong. Finally, I turned into a side hall and sank to the cold tile floor in front of a bank of lockers.

"Now," I panted, "where no one can see." Suddenly the grownup facade was gone. My I'm-in-complete-control front vanished into the dark hallway. The anger I was so full of melted into total helplessness. Curled up next to those lockers I was no longer a seventeen-year-old, six-foot-tall high school senior. I was hurt. I was crying. In the darkness I pulled my knees tight against my chest like a lost, forsaken child. I wiped my face on the pant leg of my best suit.

What had happened? This was not how I had dreamed it every night for so many weeks. I was supposed to have rushed up to receive the award. I was supposed to stand on the first-place platform — me! What had happened? I leaned my head back against the steel lockers and stared into the empty black beyond the window.

"Here he is!" the announcer had said. "This year's top student. The best our state has to offer." I remember tapping my foot nervously. "Come on, say it," I had thought, already moving forward in my chair.

"This year's winner is. . . ." The announcer cleared his throat. "Ladies and gentlemen, may I present ____________ ________________."

My stomach tightened again as I remembered the feeling that had engulfed me at that moment. The acceptance speech, which was already on the tip of my tongue, catapulted backward, burning its way through my entire body. Finally it settled, sick and sour, like a bowl of raw pancake batter, right in the center of my chest. My brain was numb. My throat was dry.

"Someone correct that man," was my frantic thought. "He's blowing it on live TV!" Why was everyone applauding? He had announced the wrong name.

A tree branch swished the window in front of me, startling me out of my trance. Everything was still so vivid. No, this wasn't how I had dreamed it at all. I was there. I was ready, sitting on the stage in my best suit. Who missed his cue? Who let the final curtain fall just as the spotlight was supposed to hit me, center stage?

I thought of the indignity, the dishonesty. "It isn't fair," I sighed. The four years of preparation I had made for this contest all came flooding back to me. "How could they pass it by?" I whispered. "How could those judges have overlooked everything?"

I stood and leaned limply against the metal-cold lockers. I just didn't feel right about their decision. "Of course you don't," I told myself. "You lost!"

But that wasn't it. It was deeper than that. I had lost before and felt right about it. But tonight, as much as I wanted and needed to, I couldn't reconcile the judgment with the facts. An injustice had been done, and I was the victim.

I wiped my eyes with the back of my hand and moved along the lonely hall. Where did I go wrong? I hadn't prayed for victory. I had just prayed that the judges would be honest and fair. I had done it right!

I had decided what was best for me. I had done the right thing. I had the right reasons. I even had multi-motives, didn't I?

When I turned the corner near the trophy case, Carolyn saw me. "Brad," she came running up to me and clutched my arm. "Where have you been? I've looked everywhere!" I forced a smile. Carolyn Grow had won the award last year, and she had now come back to haunt me with her beauty, her self-control, and her winning. At least that's what I thought at the time. Now I know what a world of good, honest caring can do.

"It hurts," I confessed. "It really hurts."

After a long minute Carolyn put her arm in mine and we started walking.

"It always hurts to lose, Brad. You know that."

"You won, Carolyn."

"Won what?" she asked quickly. "The money? Two hundred and fifty dollars. Big deal. I could have earned more at a steady job."

"The title, Carolyn," I whispered painfully. "The recognition."

Carolyn spoke again. "You know you deserved that award."

"But no one else does," I said, saturating myself in my own pity.

"They do, too." Carolyn's voice sounded irritated. "The important ones do. The people you care about, and the ones who care about you. They all know."

We sat on some folding chairs.

"Everything I have done," I said, "every service project, every award, every effort was aimed at this."

Carolyn just listened. "I worked so hard. Two months I slaved on that portfolio, alone. Two solid months, and it was all for nothing." I stiffened suddenly at what I had just said.

I think Carolyn began to talk, but I can't remember. The only clear thing in my mind was the word I had just said. Nothing! But wait, I'm the one with multi-motives, remember? I'm the one who did it right.

How often I had said to Mr. Roylance, "This portfolio is a fantastic personal history, contest or no contest."

Carolyn's words shook me. ". . . And Brad," she said, "aren't you grateful that a contest like this pushes you into making a record like your portfolio? I mean, think how important that will be to your kids."

"Multi-motives," I thought. "I had them. I represented my school. I met new friends." Why was I still disappointed? Why did I feel that I'd wasted everything for nothing? Where was the satisfaction multi-motives were supposed to provide?

Wasn't I supposed to find joy in participation? Now I was more confused than ever. This scholarship program hadn't worked, and multi-motives hadn't worked either.

Carolyn stood up and made ready to go. "You don't need a title, believe me. In one year no one even remembers there was a contest.

"Except me," I responded softly. "I'll never forget."

Sometimes I wonder if the person who wrote "Time heals all wounds" ever lost the top scholar award. I have never forgotten that night. Not because of the contest — Carolyn was completely right about that, bless her. The minute I stopped flattering myself with the thought that others are so concerned with every detail of my life, I forgot all about the contest, the scholarship money, and losing. Surprisingly, it didn't even matter when it came to light that the judge had been mistaken and had never looked at the portfolios at all. I remember that night because that's the moment I forced myself to analyze this idea I had labeled "multi-motives."

I did come to realize what I had done wrong. It wasn't with a dramatic flash of lightning and the Tabernacle Choir's singing "Battle Hymn of the Republic." In fact, I can't pinpoint a day and say, "That's when I learned this marvelous thing." The realization of my mistake came gradually, until one night, I just knew.

It was while touring with the musical, "My Turn on Earth." We had just completed a performance in Atlanta, Georgia. That night I recorded the following in my journal:

"October 13th (Friday the 13th!), Roger's wedding day at the Provo Temple. I can't believe it! My older brother married this soon after his mission! I would like to be home today, but that's impossible.

"Georgia is beautiful. Everyone has been nice to us. I'm grateful for good people everywhere working to live the gospel. The Young Adult group in one of the stakes here took our cast and crew out to dinner tonight at a super-nice restaurant in town. I ordered crepes. They're great. I wonder if we could figure out how to make them at home! Well, anyway, one of the girls at the dinner knew a friend back home who had worked in the top scholar award contest a few years ago. It really brought up some old memories.

"I figured something out about all that. Multi-motives do work! When they are used honestly, that is. I kept saying I had multi-motives (in my personal record or when meeting people, and so on), but what I really had were excuses I could use if I didn't win. That's why I was crushed and said, 'All that work for nothing.' If they had truly been motives, I'd have been working just as hard to make that portfolio, as a record of my life, as I was working to win the scholarship. Instead, I plugged along with the single, weakest motive of all — to win. Everything else was an excuse in case someone should ask me why I was doing all this. For instance, I didn't really care about meeting new friends, but I thought it sounded better to say, 'It's fun meeting new people,' instead of 'I'm out to win this thing, and anyone who gets in my way is going to get barubas in his face.' Well, anyway, it feels good to have figured it all out.

"I have to laugh at myself now for getting so uptight about a contest. When you put it all into proper perspective, an eternal perspective, the growth is what matters, and the happiness that comes through trying. I wonder why I let the contest mean everything at the time.

"I hope I can always remember what I've learned out of all this and try to use multi-motives honestly, because I know they'll work if I let them.

"It's great to be young and LDS: and it's great to be busy (I have to keep telling myself that). Tomorrow we leave for Florida."

Dishonest motives, right thing/wrong reason, wrong thing/right reason, are all detour paths that might be going up the mountain, but which curve and twist so much that I never can figure them out. But when I do the right thing for the right reason I'm on a secure, straight-ahead path that's pointing upward for sure.

5

There's a Libyan Soccer Player In My Shower

It was the end of June, and the summer was just beginning to level off to the sometimes what-shall-I-do-now stage. I had just finished sixth grade and, with my twelve-year-old mind, had decided that now, being a man, I needed to start making my own way in life.

Mentally, I reviewed my regular odd jobs. I could tend at the neighbor's, but all I ever got from that were homemade sweetrolls. "Dad likes me to work in our yard and around the house," I thought. But again, the only pay was an occasional movie. It seemed Grandma was the only one who ever gave cash money, but only on my birthday, and that was still six months away.

"This is terrible," I sighed, flopping down on the grassy hill behind the house. "I'm twelve years old, and I need a job."

I picked myself up from the soft grass and ran to the back porch where Roger, my fifteen-year-old brother, was pumping up his bike tires. "This is serious," I explained. "I mean, what about dates, and gas for the car?" Roger stopped pumping to stare at me.

"You're only twelve."

"But prices are going up, Rog. I've got to start saving now."

No one seemed to grasp the seriousness of my situation. I

was desperate. It was the end of June, which left only two months in which to earn my life savings before school began again.

Every night for the next four days I scanned the want ads. "Wanted: strong healthy boy, eager to work. Good pay. Must be sixteen or over." Sixteen, sixteen! Why didn't they want me? Sixteen sounded too old to be able to work very hard anyway.

Finally, after about a week, it happened. I found the perfect job. I was just finishing a Yahtzee game with Roger when the doorbell rang. It was his turn to play, so I jumped up from the rug and dashed to the door.

"Hello," I smiled.

"Hi, there, young man!" It was Mr. Mangleson, the farmer who operated the cherry orchards across the highway from our place. He stretched out his rough hand, and I shook it eagerly. "Is your older brother here?"

"You mean Rog?"

"That's the one," he replied.

Without taking my eyes from his deeply wrinkled face, I yelled, "Hey, Rog, come quick."

After the two said hello, I lingered down the hall where I could still hear every word.

"Well, Roger, have you thought about it? I'm paying four cents a pound this year."

"I have. I'd be glad to come over and pick."

"That's great," Mr. Mangleson nodded. "I always need good pickers in my orchard."

Why hadn't I thought of it before? I turned and hurried into the next room. Cherry picking, that's perfect! Four cents a pound would be four dollars a day if I picked a hundred pounds, which I figured I could easily do if I worked till six o'clock every night. He wouldn't even have to teach me how to pick, because I had helped before at the stake farm and in Grandma's trees. (Of course, I couldn't climb very high when she was around, but once when I was picking alone I got a whole bucket off the very top branch.)

I ran to the closet near the back door and pulled out Mom's old metal bucket. "Yep, this is the one." I carried it quickly to the bathroom scale.

"If I get four cents a pound. . . ." I balanced it carefully so I could still see the numbers. "Wow!" I'd earned twelve cents and there wasn't even a cherry in it yet.

That night, everything I dreamed was round and red and juicy. The thing I wanted to do most in the whole world was to pick cherries.

After lunch the following day I finally finished hoeing my share of the family garden and emptying the garbage. Then I rushed to my bedroom to get ready.

The decision on which suit to wear was easy, since I only had one. But it was new. I had gotten it when I became a deacon, only six months earlier. I just knew that would impress him. With Dad's comb I parted my hair meticulously, and I wetted it until every strand was glued perfectly in place. Then, with no time to lose, I ran to the front door and threw it open. The late afternoon breeze rearranged the hair I had so neatly combed. My broad smile slowly faded into disappointment. He wasn't anywhere in sight. I shut the door and sat with my back against the wall, waiting, and waiting, and waiting. Finally, when the hall clock bonged seven times, I opened the door again. Where was he? Where was Mr. Mangleson?

The following day I repeated the whole ritual. "I really need this job," I told myself. "Why won't he come and ask me?" Late that night, a very disappointed deacon crawled under his single summer blanket.

When Mom came in to say goodnight I was still awake.

"I'd be a good cherry picker, Mom. Honest I would." Mom sat on the end of my bed while I explained the whole thing from the beginning. When I was finished, she looked at me and said simply, "Why don't you ask him for a job?"

"Oh, Mom," I moaned. She had confirmed my belief that the older generation knew very little. "That's just not how it's done. I know these things, Mom. I was there when Mr. Mangleson came and asked Roger."

"Does Mr. Mangleson know you'd like a job?"

"He knew Roger wanted one, didn't he?"

Mom laughed. "Because Roger phoned him the other night."

I was so embarrassed I didn't know what to say. Mom stood, smiled, and pushed the sheet tightly around my chin. A

June breeze shook lightly through the screen on my bedroom window. "If this job is something you want, Brad, and you've got the self-motivation, the first move is up to you. Let's call Mr. Mangleson first thing tomorrow."

That sixth-grade summer was my first encounter with the marvel of self-motivation. The chance to pick cherries was too choice an opportunity to just let fly by. "If it's something you want, the first move is up to you." In her own way Mom really made a profound impact on me. Too often I end up like a Buckingham Palace guard stationed stoically outside my guardhouse watching opportunities, like tourists, running toward me, staring me in the face, and then passing me by.

Honest motivation from within is by far the strongest incentive for self-betterment.

WITH UPTURNED CUP

Elusive opportunities,
Nebulous as shifting storm clouds,
Burst upon me momentarily.

Will my cup be turned up
To receive
A
    single
        raindrop?

The surest, most secure way to keep my cup turned up, as I said in this poem, is by depending upon self-motivation to do it.

I have always had a partial awareness of the importance of inner motivation, but I realized its full value after graduating from high school. I lived for two months on the third floor of a decaying dormitory named, quite fittingly, Gravely Hall. Each morning I would wake up, scare the cockroaches out of my way, and trot down the hall to the showers.

After the first few days this became a ritual I dreaded, because the shower was always ice cold. Nevertheless, every morning, in I would jump, until one day I woke late and, upon entering the dorm bathroom, discovered a visiting soccer player from Libya in my cold shower. With no time to lose, I turned to another one. When I reached my hand to test the water, I couldn't believe what I felt. Warmth! Heat! It had been there all along only one shower stall away.

Despite my being late, I let the heavenly hot water run. What luxury to be *enjoying* a shower for the first time all summer. In the next stall my Libyan friend complained in broken English, "Dis showah is berry, berry cold!"

"You just have to try another one," I yelled, laughing at myself. Why hadn't I done that the first day?

It seems I'm always getting caught up in my own uncomfortable routines until someone forces me to turn on the hot water. The question I am beginning to ask myself now is, "Why wait? Why wait to find a Libyan soccer player in my shower?"

If I'm not happy and progressing where I am, trying what I'm trying, I don't have to vegetate in a cold shower for the rest of my life. I can find incentive within myself to step out and move ahead.

That summer I learned a lot about self-motivation because it was the first time in my life that I was totally alone and completely in control. Suddenly Dad wasn't there to waken me for priesthood meeting; and if I missed Sunday School, nobody knew me well enough to care. I was the only one who knew if I ate all my carrots and peas. I could sleep when I wanted, eat when I wanted. I can't remember a time when my spare time was really all mine, as it was in Gravely Hall. Of course, I had to fulfill my responsibility to the summer theater that hired me. Performing six nights a week, rehearsing every day, and building various sets kept me busy; but when the rehearsal was over, whatever I did was entirely up to me.

The motivation to wash my clothes and keep my dorm room clean had to come from inside. I found it too easy to say, "These pants will do for another week"; or, "Who'll know if I sleep in till noon?" It was a daily test to dig up the drive to live as I knew I should, a test I had to pass.

As a young Latter-day Saint entering our jet-propelled world, which I've been warned is slipping full speed into degradation, I'll be relying more and more on those motivations from within. After all, who else around me at the time will care if I'm morally clean or trying to be honest?

"Come on, Brad, just have a sip. Your bishop's not even here to slap your hand." I had heard it all in the seminary filmstrips and had laughed. "That never happens in real life," my friends and I would say. "What a joke!"

But when it happened that summer to me, it was no joke. I was living my own personal seminary filmstrip. They were right. No one would see; no one would know — *except* Heavenly Father and me, the two most important of all.

"When I was young," Brother Taylor, a grandfather-aged friend told me, "I could never have found a dirty magazine if I had wanted to. Now, it seems, they're right there on the store shelves, plain as day, sitting right next to the *Reader's Digest* or *Boys' Life*."

In our supersonic world of accepted abortion, divorce, dishonesty, inflation, war, hate, even homosexuality and child abuse, where does the motivation come from to try to better ourselves? to stay away from the R-rated films, not to drink, not to lie? Where will the motivation come from that will stop me from shoplifting, vandalizing, or breaking any of the commandments?

In my life it hasn't come from my Church leaders, my friends, or even my parents, though they have all helped. The incentive to keep moving upward on the mountain to perfection comes, and must come, from within.

6

A Ten-gallon Attitude

The buzz ripped through me like a paper cut. Six o'clock came early. I fly-swatted at the annoying alarm clock. It took me a moment to realize where I was. "Just five more minutes," I yawned, rolling toward the mud-orange colored wall of what otherwise would have been a nice hotel room.

It was the middle of my senior year. I was representing Boy Scouts of America as a delegate in the Report to the Nation. I knew it was a great opportunity, but right then I wanted to forget opportunity and make up the sleep I'd lost the night before. I pulled the skinny blanket tightly over my right shoulder and tried to remember the dream I was having before that obnoxious travel alarm stole the scene.

"Rise and shine! Rise and shine!" The thick Texas accent was almost harder to take than the alarm. His name was Robert. He was my assigned roommate. I didn't even have to open my eyes to know that he was showered, shaved, and dressed, and had probably reorganized the entire city of New York already that morning. I had always pictured Texans with ten-gallon hats; instead, Rob had a ten-gallon voice.

"Rise and shine!"

"Just five more minutes," I pleaded.

"Five more minutes!" he yahooed. "You could be showered and halfway dressed in five more minutes."

Finally I forced my right eye open. "Who painted this room orange?"

Rob laughed. "That's to wake you up."

"Or kill me off." I sat up and rubbed my head.

"Come on, Brad, up and at 'em!"

I've decided there is nothing more irritating than an up-and-at-'em at 6:05 A.M. except maybe a rise-and-shine at 6:00 A.M. Rob was already in the bathroom starting my shower.

"Better hurry, buddy, you know how fast that hot water goes."

"Some buddy!" I growled. But it did get me out of bed and into the shower in almost a single bound. Rob was right. The hot water went fast and suddenly. While I washed my face, instant ice. All I could do was fumble to turn it off because the hotel soap was gouging into my eye.

"Rotten!" I yelled. "What a rotten day!"

"No, Brad," came the Texas drawl, "it's a great day."

I searched blindly around the bathroom for a towel. My eye was still doing cartwheels because of that soap.

"It's all in the attitude, mah boy. Oh, by the way, there was only one towel, so I guess you can use that extra roll of toilet tissue."

With such a negative beginning, how could I know that would be the day that I would meet Dr. Norman Vincent Peale, "Mr. Positive Thinking" himself.

"Dr. Peale didn't invent positive thinking," our Report to the Nation director told us, "but he popularized it with such books as his *The Power of Positive Thinking*." I fought to stay awake as the adviser continued. Our bus chugged criss-cross through the traffic of the tight, crowded city streets.

"Oh, excuse me," Rob said. Mysteriously the corner of his briefcase had lodged itself in my side.

"I'll only be bruised for life — nothing to worry about," I replied.

Rob was whispering so as not to disturb our adviser, who had strayed off into a world of his own, discoursing on a garbage strike or some other modern phenomenon.

"I thought you'd be interested in the books Mr. Johnson was just talking about." Rob flicked the briefcase flap open.

"I knew it," I said. "You just happen to have every one."

"Fresh from the library back home." As he smiled I began

counting his teeth. "I knew we were going to meet him, so I checked out every book to be had."

"Meet him?" I jerked awake. "Meet Dr. Peale?"

"Sure. Didn't you read your schedule today?"

"Yes, but. . . ." I turned sideways toward him. "I thought we were just going to some church."

"Some church!" Rob repeated. "The Marble Collegiate Church, you know, where Dr. Peale is the minister."

"Oh, yes, that church!" I still didn't really understand, but I sounded convincing enough that Rob turned back to his books.

"Now, this one's my favorite." He handed me *Enthusiasm Makes the Difference*. "There are good quotes on pages 13, 20, 21, 28. . . ."

"Slow down." I flipped to a page he mentioned. "What's so neat?"

"It's where he quotes Jack London, in the middle of the page."

Following my finger turned out to be the only way to keep my place as the bus jarred its way across New York. I had never thought of Rob as a bookworm, but there was his briefcase, full of Dr. Peale's books, still jabbing my side and proving me wrong.

"Haven't you found it yet?" Rob leaned across and began reading out loud.

"I can find it." I pulled the book so close to my face that I couldn't read it, but neither could Rob, and that's all that mattered right then. "Wait, here it is. 'The proper function of man is to live, not to exist.' Is that the one?"

"Yeah." Rob was speaking with a pen clamped tightly in his teeth. "Now read down to where it talks about fighting obstacles and enjoying every minute of it."

"Where's that?" I asked. Reading on buses had always made me sick.

"It's right there after that part that says, 'It's a strange, sad fact that many individuals exist yet are not really living.' "

"Isn't that what I just read?"

"No, it's another part."

"Do you have this whole book memorized?"

Rob laughed. "I wish. Oh, and when you get done there,

check the 'as if' principle on page 20. You can't meet Norman Vincent Peale without reading the 'as if' principle."

Mr. Johnson apparently had exhausted his knowledge of garbage and how it struck, and he now walked back toward us. "What's all this jabbering about? Is everything all right here?"

"Fine." Sometimes Rob's drawl seemed too much to be true. "Just fine and dandy."

The whole group watched as Mr. Johnson cleaned his glasses. At last, when he was safely back in his seat and absorbed this time in the evils of inflation, I turned to page 20; and, motion sickness or not, I began to read.

"Many years ago a noted psychologist, William James, announced his famous 'as if' principle. He said, 'If you want a quality, act as if you already had it.' "

"Have you found it yet, huh?" I liked to do a lot of things with Rob but after questions like that, reading wasn't one of them.

"Yes, I just read it."

"That's the best! Isn't it great where he says, 'Start visualizing yourself not as you think you are, but rather as you'd like to be'?"

"Sure, Rob, it's a good thought, but it's nothing new."

"Course it isn't." I think he was getting frustrated that I wasn't absorbing all this knowledge with proper appreciation. "Haven't you ever heard what Max Reinhardt said, 'Always act the part and you can become whatever you wish to become.' "

"You *are* a bookworm!"

Rob grinned. "No, I just think all this stuff is important to know — because it's all in the attitude, mah boy. It's like . . . well, all my life everyone has usually seen me exactly the way I see myself."

"How well I know what you mean," I said. "When my self-image is poor and I'm mentally in a bottomless pit, and everyone who passes can't resist pointing out some new mountain range on my complexion, it's murder to look into the mirror and smile as I should, you know what I mean? On days like that it's hard to say honestly, 'I'm on top,' or as Dr. Peale says in his book, 'I can do all things through Christ, which strengtheneth me' (Philippians 4:13). And whenever I do say stuff like that, I never change anyway."

"Now, I'm not Dr. Peale." My Texan authority leaned forward in his seat. "But I'd say the reason nothing changes is that you're only doing half of what you need to. You're seeing yourself on top, or at least that's what you say you're doing, but you are not *being* yourself on top. Remember, if you want a quality, act as if you already have it."

Mr. Johnson raised his voice, "We're almost there, people." Mechanically, he began reviewing the niceties of behavior. "This is the famous Marble Collegiate Church. We will be sitting in a reserved. . . ."

"Psst. Brad, I know a girl back home who just kinda slides down the hall at school. I didn't even know what she looked like until a while ago, because she always carried her books smashed into her face, I mean flat on her nose."

"I know the type." We both joined the aisle line which was forming in the bus.

Rob went on: "One day I talked to her at lunch and she said, 'I want to be involved and outgoing.' So I told her what Dr. Peale says about — wait, it's right here." He fumbled quickly through his case and handed me *The Power of Positive Thinking*. "You find it while I put this dumb case together. Page 16 or 17, I think."

I read out loud so he could hear, too. " 'Formulate and stamp on your mind a mental picture of yourself succeeding. Hold this picture tenaciously. Never permit it to fade. Your mind will seek to develop this picture.' "

"That's it." Rob stepped off the bus ahead of me. "That's what I told this girl. And you know what she said?" I marveled at how Rob could say so many words so fast and still be understood, even with his accent.

"Huh, you know what she said? She said, 'I have a picture.' Well, I was absolutely stumped. Right then I decided that seeing is only a step to being. So I said, 'Well, Honey, if you can see yourself as a confident involved person, then there's nothing stopping you from being that way.' "

"Maybe there was, Rob," I said.

Mr. Johnson, who had gone into the church, now came outside. We began to gather about him for instructions. I continued, "Maybe she doubted herself and felt insecure from childhood, or something."

"Then she could go and see the counselor and learn the origin of those feelings. After all, like it says in the book, 'Self-knowledge leads to a cure.' Come to think of it, I should have said that to her, too, huh?"

Mr. Johnson walked between us. "You boys be quiet now." We entered the church, and the usher led us down the carpeted aisle to our seats.

"It's a beautiful building," I whispered to Rob, who was studying the face of each choir member.

"I like being up front," he approved.

While we waited quietly for the service to begin, I kept thinking about what Rob had told me. It was all familiar but I had never analyzed it before.

"Look how full this place is getting." Rob had twisted around and was noticing the back balcony. "What do you think he'll talk about?"

"Dr. Peale?" I asked. "Oh, maybe what it says in that book, about how positive thinking is just an extension of faith. What do you think he'll speak on?"

"I don't know, but I'll tell you what I hope he says." Mr. Johnson glared our way. I signaled Rob to keep it down. "I want him to tell us about attitude."

Rob thought for a second. "Once I read, not in one of Peale's books, but I read about how 90 percent of every skill development is attitude. Think of the things I could do!"

Again I reminded him to whisper before Mr. Johnson gave us another death look.

"Wasn't it William James who said something like, 'The greatest discovery of my generation is that human beings can alter their lives by altering their attitudes of mind'?"

Even though I didn't know, I was flattered that he thought I did.

"I hope he talks on that," Rob went on. "Changing attitudes, that's what I 'd like to learn about today — because it's all in the attitude."

"Learn? What more do you need to learn?" The meeting was beginning. "No offense to Dr. Peale, but I think you should be up there speaking."

Rob grinned broadly. I really was beginning to appreciate him. He'd wormed his positive way right into my life.

As the meeting went forward, I must confess that I didn't listen intently; too many loose ideas still floated in my mind: altering attitudes, act the part, believe in yourself. I had always thought of myself as a positive thinker, and I always was one until something went wrong. But Dr. Peale calls it "a simple, workable philosophy of living," not a pastime for Brad Wilcox when there's nothing else to occupy his brain.

Finally, after a stirring number by the choir, Dr. Peale faced the congregation. His gray hair was combed straight back and the light through the church windows reflected in the glasses he was wearing. He didn't look old. He looked strong. After a pause, he raised his left arm and pointed to the balcony.

"You." His smile was broad. His full voice was deep, and it rang through the silent gathering. "You can change things — for sure."

After the meeting, Rob said, "I felt like a sponge trying to soak up ever word."

As for me, I was still speechless. Mr. Johnson led our small group to a lounge at the rear of the church.

Rob went on, "Did you hear when he was talking about the damage we do by saying, 'I can't'?"

All I could do was nod at him, remembering back to when I had first learned that lesson. It was as a Boy Scout trying to reach the rank of Eagle. I recall looking at the long list of requirements for each of the endless merit badges and declaring, "I can't do all this." My leaders said, "Yes, you can." I said, "I can't." My parents said, "Yes, you can." I whimpered, "I can't." Each merit badge I needed to get had requirements I was sure I could never complete.

Spouting and splashing and floundering awkwardly in the swimming pool while trying to earn, of all things, a life-saving merit badge is when it came to me that no human being was born in the water. Everyone had to *learn* to swim, *learn* to dive, *learn* life-saving techniques. What a flash of basic revelation in my young life!

Feeling supremely confident in my new discovery, I climbed out of the water and ran dripping and sloshing to the diving board. "I *can* do it!" I yelled. With a one-two-three-go, in I dived, executing a resounding belly flop which will be remembered as causing a minor tidal wave in the local pool. "I can't do it," I muttered, crawling out of the water. No, I couldn't do it, but I realized that I could *learn* to do it. I could commit myself and work until I dived well enough for that merit badge requirement.

"I can't." I've said those words all my life. "I can't swim, I can't cook, I can't manage money, I can't speak before an audience, I can't climb the rope." Of course I can't. I wasn't born with skills. I was born with the capacity to develop the skills I desire and the intelligence to try. Now, each time I see a skill performed, I remind myself, "That kid wasn't born singing on Broadway. It took interest, time, practice and work."

Rob was pacing the lounge in his excitement. "Brad, didn't you love it when he quoted Romans 8:31? 'If God be for us, who can be against us?' What a scripture! And Matthew 17:20? Wasn't that fantastic?"

"Was that the one about faith?" In trying so hard to remember everything, I seemed to be remembering nothing.

Rob opened a Bible which sat on a round wooden table in the middle of the room. " 'If ye have faith . . . nothing shall be impossible unto you.' "

"But faith without works," I reminded.

"I guess it comes down to what we were talking about on the bus, Brad."

I didn't quite understand. "You mean, seeing yourself in a certain way as a step to *becoming* that way?"

"Right!" Rob grinned. "I guess when I say, 'I can,' it's only a step then to saying, 'I will.' "

Mr. Johnson grouped us around the polished table. "We can go into Dr. Peale's office now. If anyone has a camera and would like me to take a picture, just leave the. . . ."

"What a great pair," I thought. " 'I can, I will.' Think of the things that have been accomplished when those two phrases have been coupled. Alone, neither of them carries much clout, but when they are combined, the product can be magnificent."

Mr. Johnson reviewed the proper protocol for young people in our situation, and I kept thinking ahead. "Every miraculous discovery during my lifetime started at the same point," I told myself. "In fact, every good thing that has ever been accomplished in the world began with people saying, 'I can, I will,' people believing in their goals and abilities, people with faith in God and in themselves."

Rob walked beside me into the impressive office. "What do you think he'll say when he shakes your hand?"

"I don't know," I whispered back. "Probably, 'Hello.' "

"Not Dr. Peale. I think he'll quote Henry Ford and say, 'If you think you can, or think you can't, you're right.' Or maybe he'll. . . ." The door closed behind us. I felt chilled with excitement.

I had met great men before, leaders and dignitaries who have influenced the world, but rarely do I meet the great men who influence my personal world. And that day, with Rob's help, Dr. Norman Vincent Peale had done just that.

His office proved to be long and narrow. At one side were the double doors through which we entered; at the other, a bay window and his desk. In between was the largest collection of pictures, plaques and certificates of award I had ever seen. Frames covered the walls from the carpet to five feet above my head, with pictures and letters from presidents, kings, his friends both famous and little known.

Rob nudged me when he noticed the certificate issued from Brigham Young University. "Isn't that in Utah?" he asked quietly.

"You bet!"

Dr. Peale smiled broadly as Mr. Johnson introduced us. "This is the Report to the Nation Delegation," he announced. Dr. Peale spoke to the entire group for a while, then began to shake our hands "good-bye."

"What if Rob is right?" I wondered. "What if he says something profound?"

Eventually he stood before me. The top of his head reached my chin. "Hello, " he laughed.

"Hello," I responded enthusiastically. I was right. There were no quotes or eternal truths, just a handshake and a warm "hello" which was profound and positive enough for me.

At the end of that ten days on the East Coast, I stood in the airport in Washington, D.C., with my coat over one arm, my suitcase in my hand, and a difficult task in front of me: saying good-bye to Rob.

"If y'all are ever down in Texas, just look me up." It had been hard to get used to his accent, yet now I was missing it even before we parted.

"Good luck," I said.

"Aw, Brad, I know people are fond of saying that, and I know you mean well, but we don't need luck. The Lord has given us all the gifts we need." He reached over and thumped my chest. "They're all right there, just waiting to be called into action."

"You'll never let a chance go by, will you, Rob?"

"No sireee!" His expression was sincere.

"Next to Norman Vincent Peale," I said, "you're the positivest positive thinker I know."

"Flight 201 now boarding at Gate 7A," the P.A. system interrupted.

Rob shifted his feet. "You've got to go, so I'll say good-bye." He stretched out his hand.

"Rob, you keep going like you are now, and someday you'll be president." He smiled knowingly. I gaped as the realization hit me.

"Rob, you're not. . . ." I peered deeply into his eyes. What I had said as a joke, wasn't. "You're not seriously going to be — I mean, you're not thinking about. . . ."

"Flight 201 now boarding at Gate 7A."

Rob flashed me one last two-acre Texas smile. "It's all in the attitude, mah boy, it's all in the attitude."

7

May I Have This Dance?

"All right, all you boys. There are lots of girls who would love to dance, so let's get busy." Our tour adviser looked directly at Jason and me and then turned on the record player again. A tropical breeze shuffled through leaves in a planter behind us on the hotel patio.

I had only just finished eighth grade and didn't even know how to dance by myself, let alone ask a girl to do it with me.

"I guess we should go dance, Brad." Jason was rolling up the embroidered sleeves of his I'm-a-tourist-in-Mexico shirt he had bought that afternoon.

"No, not me."

"But Mr. Jarman said there are girls who want to dance, and anyway this is the last night of the tour and we'll probably never see them again." A sudden gust blew Jason's hair across his eyes. Casually he brushed it back again.

This educational tour through Mexico had been sponsored by our school district, and up to now it had been a great experience. Why did they have to spoil it with a dance?

"Come on." Jason got me to my feet. "You ask Joan, and I'll ask Christie." He buttoned his top shirt button, moved across the patio, and offered his hand. "Hey, Christie, would you like to dance?"

I stood back and watched in hopes of gaining instant learning in the intricacies of social interaction.

Christie flipped her hair. "Gee . . . ah . . . thanks Jason, but not right now."

"What about you, Joan?" he asked.

From my safe position behind the lines, I noticed Jason's crooked-tooth smile. I saw my friend for the first time as those girls might be seeing him, and I guess, overall, he did look kind of unusual.

"I'd really like to dance, Jason, but I don't like this song."

He tugged at his gaudy new shirt. "Well, maybe later?"

The two embarrassed girls looked quickly at each other. "Oh . . . ah . . . we're not feeling too well."

After a moment he came back to me. "Okay, Brad, who should we ask next?"

I still couldn't believe what Joan had said. "Not feeling well!" I complained to Jason. "She felt well enough to dance with Monroe a few minutes ago."

"But he's a senior in high school. We're only eighth graders."

"Ninth grade now," I reminded him. I followed him to the tile fountain in the center of the patio, where Stephanie LeBette stood. With her hand on her hip and her nose in the air, she might as well have been a water-spouting statue.

I realized what Jason was about to do even before he said, "Hey, Stephanie, how about a dance?"

"Jason, don't. . . ." I turned away with elaborate casualness. Stephanie broke her pose to smile disdainfully and glide haughtily away.

"Well, how about it, you want to dance?" Jason called after her.

"No, gracias, Señor." She didn't even bother to look back.

I pushed a ripple into the fountain pool. "I don't get it, Jas. I thought girls liked to dance."

"They do," he assured me. "Look, why don't *you* ask Stephanie?"

"No way, not her. I don't want to get turned down, too."

With his square fingers Jason jarred the water again, contorting our shadowed reflections.

"Brad, if Stephanie doesn't want to dance it's her problem, not yours."

"But if she said no, why keep asking her?"

"Why not?"

The director turned up the music again. Jason stepped closer to me to be heard. "Why should you let *her* decide how you're going to act?" He touched his greased hair, which was unmoved since the last time. "I'm going over there and ask some new girls. Want to come?"

I shook my head and sat on the tile rim. Even through my thick jeans it felt cold. Jason walked away, stepping awkwardly to the musical beat.

As I think back on the incident, I realize that Jason is one of the few people I've ever known who *acts* toward people. Most of us *react* to people. He knew what he wanted and how he should behave. If Stephanie had refused me like that, I'd have either crawled off and buried myself in a Mexican pyramid or said, "You're not so neat yourself, you goat," and maybe bitten her ankle or something.

I remember that evening as though I were a character in a cartoon sitting by that cold fountain thinking, but with nothing written in my thought bubble. If I were to fill it in now, I guess I'd write, "No one is more miserable than the dummy who always reacts."

At that long-ago dance my center of confidence was outside myself, being kicked around that patio like an old can. If Christie had said, "You're cold," I'd have sneezed. If Monroe had said, "You're hot," I'd have wiped my forehead. My feelings toward the whole situation were totally dependent upon a few people who could decide if I were to be embarrassed or proud, rude or gracious, introverted or extroverted. Unlike Jason, whose emotional security was rooted within himself as it should be, I had relinquished control of my own personality.

I'm thankful for that skinny tourist friend and for the important principle he personified: to act and not to react. For in all the dances I've attended since that bomb-out in Mexico, not once have I bitten Stephanie LeBette's ankle (or even any other girl's).

If I realize that some particular way of thinking or acting could make me a better person, and if I realize that the capacity to do it is right inside me, then what holds me back?

After I'm thinking positively, what stops me from determining to take the next step and commit myself?

In the middle of my sophomore year, my high school drama department announced auditions for the annual Shakespeare play. "This is great!" I thought. I pictured myself in colorful Elizabethan costume playing a rousing Shakespearean role, and I got all whipped up. It was something I had wanted to do all year, so between American History class and lunch I ran into the office and picked up a dittoed sheet of dialogue.

> What early tongue so sweet saluteth me? —
> Young son, it argues a distemper'd head
> So soon to bid good morrow to thy bed.
>
> –*Romeo and Juliet*

"That sure doesn't sound like English to me," I thought, reading through the rest of the tryout material. I couldn't make sense of what was going on or of how I was supposed to say one word. I'd seen Shakespearean plays before, and even movies. The lines had always sounded easy and natural.

"What's wrong with you?" I asked myself. The audition line I had joined after school was getting shorter. I stood in the C-wing stairwell and nervously reread the pages. "What early tongue. . . ." I was growing frantic.

Matt Ricks filed into the line behind me. "Hey, Brad, it's good to see you trying out."

I didn't speak. I couldn't. Matt was the best actor in the school, and I was in awe.

"Oh boy!" I thought. "Now I'll really look like a fool when he tries out after me. Well, I don't have to look like a fool. I'm not going to walk out on that stage and make a total idiot of myself." I turned away from the audition line and walked quickly to my hall locker. Luckily Matt was surrounded by his usual harem of admirers and didn't notice me leave.

I argued with myself. "Don't be dumb. We've gone through all this before. Of course you might not make this play, but then, you might! You have to try." I climbed the main hall stairs to upper B wing. "You can't read Shakespearean English now, but you can learn."

Then, somehow, all the "ifs" and "theys" got to me. "Even *if* I learned it, what would *they* say *if* I botched it?" I crumpled the dialogue sheet and shoved it in my back pocket. It was easy to imagine the hateful names they might call me. It was easy to feel the hurt when they would laugh at me or whisper cruel things if I failed. I envisioned myself onstage spouting, "What early tongue so sweet saluteth me . . . ," and dodging all the pencils, spitwads, shoes, rocks, and desks that they would throw.

"I'm not trying out," I decided firmly. By now I'd missed my bus and knew I would be walking all the way home. I snatched up my books, kicked the locker door closed, and drooped back down the B-wing stairs. Why should I worry about what they would think? But I did.

I ate only one taco for dinner instead of my usual three, so Dad realized something was on my mind.

"I'm not holding myself back," I told him. "I want to try out and do what I know is best for me, but they won't let me. They're intimidating me right out of my best intentions."

"Who are *they*?" Dad asked.

"Well, you know, *they*."

"Who?" he asked again.

"The kids at school," I answered exasperatedly.

"Who?"

"You know," I fumbled. "Friends, peer group, the kids trying out who are better than me." Inside I was frantic. Not a single name came to my mind except Matt Ricks, but he was the only one I was sure wouldn't laugh.

Then, with the infallible wisdom of most fathers, Dad explained that, as people mature, it becomes less and less important what other people think or say. It took him until seven o'clock to finally convince me that "mature people are self-confident enough to live in a way that will please their Heavenly Father. They do what is best, what they know is right, regardless of what 'they' say. Some people never reach that point of maturity, while others reach it quite early in life."

He reminded me of when our family would go to the park to play baseball. The older family members would leave Chris, my younger brother, and me to play at the small baseball diamond while they went around the wire fence to the grown-ups' baseball field. "Do you remember how you two would play until you were bored, and then both of you would climb to the top of the dugout to watch the grown-ups play ball? That fence always seemed a tangible measure of age and ability. Now it can be a symbolic measure of maturity as you judge in which ballpark you'd like to play. You need to commit yourself to your goals, never caring about what 'they' may say. It is up to you to reach the fence as early in life as you can."

Before bed that night I rescued the wrinkled tryout sheet and read it over again. "What early tongue so sweet saluteth me?/Young son, it argues a distemper'd head. . . ." Finally the words were beginning to make sense. I sat right in the middle of my bedroom floor laughing out loud. "Dad's right!" I thought of where I was and imagined where I could be if I hadn't talked myself out of so many opportunities, or let others do so, without even trying. Maybe I might not have made the team, or won the office, but maybe I might have. When I was younger I didn't have the personal courage to try, so I shall never know. But that night Dad taught me that one of the nicer things about trying is that you can never lose something you don't have. You can only take a chance on winning.

Dad told me: "Trying is like climbing a hill. If you stand with your feet firmly planted at the bottom and declare that there is no way you can climb that hill, you could stand there forever. If you dare to try, you have nowhere to go but up."

My mother seems to have something written for every occasion. I like this one about:

THEY SAY

What will they think if I should dare
To choose and buy this one to wear?

They say it simply can't be done,
No point in even trying one.

I might compete and then just see —
But if I fail they'll laugh at me.

Though sometimes many, sometimes few,
It seems *they* dictate all I do.

The only thing they do not say
Is just exactly who are they!

— Val C. Wilcox

Of course it does matter what other people think and say, since we all live together on this earth. God tells me I must consider others, that I am "my brother's keeper." Actually, other people are the incentives for most good things I do. Other people and their feelings toward me are often my reward. People can inspire me to great heights, or cause me to delve dark depths. My happy balance will come as I learn to keep the opinions and actions of others in perspective. I must remember not to let others dictate my actions. In turn, I must not be the one whose remarks or actions could dominate someone else's life. We must all play in the grown-up park by acting and not reacting.

"All right," I told myself on the bedroom rug, "if *they* aren't holding me back, then what other excuse do I have? The audition is up to me." Despite the late hour, I practiced the passage again. As the Shakespearean sentences began to flow, my confidence returned. I berated myself for being so stupid as to have given other people that strong a vote in my election. Yes, other people do have a voice, and there will always be those who encourage and those who discourage; but I have free agency. I cast the deciding ballot, and I vote for what is best for me.

As I practiced, somehow Shakespeare, the man, became a reality to me. What if he had been afraid to try to write a play because of what people might think? What if he had never produced his plays because he feared being laughed at, or being called names, or being run out of town? I felt foolish. How infinitely poorer our world would be without William Shakespeare, or for that matter, without Thomas Edison, Abraham Lincoln, Harriet Tubman, and Thomas Jefferson. What if Joseph Smith had not prayed in the grove? Or then, what if he had never told anyone else about his marvelous vision of the Father and the Son, because of what "they" might (and did) think?

I would never want the Lord to say of me, "But with some I am not well pleased, for they will not open their mouths, but they hide the talent which I have given unto them, because of the fear of man. Wo unto such, for mine anger is kindled against them. And it shall come to pass, if they are not more faithful unto me, it shall be taken away, even that which they have." (D&C 60:2-3)

"Tomorrow," I vowed as I climbed into my waiting bed, "tomorrow I will really act — in more ways than one."

8

Tell 'em That for Me

The doorbell wasn't working. I knocked on the window. The lace curtains, with all the delicate little holes, the white, handmade window shade, looked like a closeup of some foreign planet. I shifted my notebook to my right hand and knocked again.

Ideas were just beginning to formulate for my next chapter — step seven, Commitment.

"Hello." Mrs. Miller opened the door wide. No one knew more about commitment than Mrs. Miller's daughter, Kelly, and that's why I was there.

Kelly Miller. I remember when the name was announced at our high school graduation. A beautiful, petite girl walked slowly across the stage. Kelly had reached a goal. It was a goal she had set for herself five years earlier. Kelly's goal was to graduate, of course, but more importantly, to walk across the stage to receive her diploma. This sounds like an ordinary sort of goal, but at the beginning of our eighth-grade year it became most extraordinary.

Kelly didn't realize I was watching her so closely that night. She couldn't know the tightness forming in my throat, but I watched and I remembered.

I remembered back to the beginning of our eighth-grade year. "Where you headed now, Kelly?" I asked. No one was used to being in school again yet.

"I have to go to P.E.," she sighed. "You know, squat-thrusts, and all that."

We turned the corner and headed down the stairs toward

the gyms. I pointed at my tennis shoes. "That's where I'm going, too."

"Great, we'll see each other all the time, then." Kelly pushed back the full brown hair which curled gently around her hand.

From the first time I met her, I always thought Kelly would have looked terrific on the cover of a teenage magazine, with her healthy good looks. She played tennis better than almost anyone in the school, and I always felt like "somebody" when we talked.

It was the end of October when Randy discovered the cracks in the partition between the girls' and the boys' gyms. Suddenly, the most exciting pastime in fifth period became watching fifty blue-uniformed eighth-grade girls do calisthenics.

"Look," Randy laughed. "Look at that one. She can't do them."

I surveyed each row of girls to discover which one he was pointing out. But the only one who wasn't going all the way down for the squat-thrust was — Kelly.

"She can't get down. She's as out of shape as you, Wilcox."

I wanted to sink a basketball in Randy's mouth, but I manfully restrained myself. I showered quickly in order to catch Kelly after class.

"What's the matter?" I asked. "Why weren't you doing squat-thrusts with the best of them?"

"Oh, do you guys look through those cracks, too?" Kelly stopped and kicked her left leg foward for inspection. "I think I sprained it, or maybe I'm just out of shape. It's stiff. Mom took me to the doctor and I passed. He says I'm just fine."

We walked along toward the lunchroom. "Of course, I guess he should check my head before he says that, huh?"

"Just give it a little rest," I advised. "The leg, I mean."

"And miss roller skating tonight?"

I weaved through the lunch line that always formed in front of my locker.

"See ya, Brad," she smiled back at me.

"See you around, Kelly." That's what I said that afternoon, but in reality it would be a long time before we'd talk again.

Rochester, Minnesota. The secretary in the school health center told me that's where she was. "In Rochester, Minnesota, at the Mayo Clinic."

I didn't understand. For all I knew, the Mayo Clinic could have been a Disneyland-type resort. It's not. And when you're there, it's not to ride the ferris wheel.

Kelly had cancer, the most deadly form of bone cancer. The secretary called it osteogenic sarcoma. Helplessly I stood there in the health center with armloads of questions which no one could answer. "That's all I know." The secretary turned back to the ringing telephone. "That's all I know."

Kelly did go roller skating after school that day; "and when she came home," her mother explained years later, "her knee looked like a basketball."

As I looked at Mrs. Miller it was easy to see where Kelly inherited her natural beauty. She brought a bowl of popcorn in from the kitchen. I opened my notebook, feeling terribly official, and began our interview.

"I was a nurse for years," Mrs. Miller continued. "So I knew something was wrong, but we had just seen the doctor. He said Kelly was fine."

I knew even after this long, that it was not easy for her to speak of it. Yet she went on calmly. "After the X ray they told us the cancer was stage four. Stage four, Brad; that's the worst it can get. Why hadn't the doctor taken an X ray the month before? The tumor looked like a second kneecap."

Kelly was flown immediately to the Mayo Clinic for further tests, but after only a few hours it was decided there was no time to test. There was no time at all. "It didn't surprise me when the doctor prepared for the amputation," Kelly said. "I didn't really care what they had to do. I just wanted to live. I've never felt a drive as strong before, and I haven't felt one since. I don't think I'm afraid of dying, but I don't want to die before my time. There's still too much I need to do here."

Her room number was 321. The hall was dark that night. A nurse stepped softly through the door with more sedatives. "I didn't take them," Kelly confessed. "I had to think. Time didn't exist for me that night. I simply lay on that bed and stared."

Kelly picked at some popcorn. "Have you ever thought

about never playing tennis again, Brad? Never running, or never even walking right for the rest of your life?"

I had no answer.

"Well, I did that night." She leaned her head back against the reclining chair and remembered. "I've never felt finality as I did that night. As much as it hurt, I slipped out of my bed to touch the floor. I had to do it one last time with both feet. I wanted to look down once more and see ten toes. I needed to spread them and feel the cold tile. My left leg was stiffer than ever; it felt like a sandbag. But Brad, that night I had to run. I knew it was the last time in this life that I would be able to do it with my real leg. It's such a simple thing. I'd never thought of running as a blessing, because it had always been natural for me, you know what I mean? But that night, it wasn't natural.

"I sneaked past the nurse's station. Pain shot through me with every step. Looking back, I couldn't have been doing anything more than hobbling, but I felt I was setting a world's record. Through the empty hall, around boxes, tables, and wheelchairs, I ran. I couldn't see where I was going in the darkened hall. My tears were falling steadily, blurring everything. I pushed myself like a child in a relay race until the agony was unbearable. Then I collapsed. I prayed. I cried. I felt tears, I mean I felt them squeezing out of all my frustration and anguish and hope and fear. My stomach knotted up. My chest was empty and shivery. Then I just cried; not a few tears trickling down my cheeks — not that kind of cry, but a sob, a choking sob."

Kelly stopped talking. For a moment I sat in empathetic silence. I was amazed at the caliber of woman who sat across from me in the small living room.

"Morning finally came," Kelly went on, "and they started the pre-op preparations. I'll always be glad that I instead of the nurse smeared all that oozy ointment stuff up and down my leg. I can't explain why I wanted to do it, but I'm glad I did, just to feel my leg, the skin, the muscle. Yeah," Kelly sighed, "I'm glad I did that."

She ate a little popcorn and offered the bowl to me. "Of course, as dreadful as the surgery was, it was like a party compared to chemotherapy."

"Tell me about it, Kel?"

"January to January, that whole year I spent a full week out of every month sick as a dog. I'd sit there for days while IV's slowly dripped into my veins. I couldn't eat anything, but still I'd throw up, and up, and up. Mom would hold the pan in front of me with her arm around my shoulders, but there was nothing to come. My hair fell out. My eyebrows fell out. My eyelashes broke off. I had sores everywhere."

"Wait," I stopped her. "You mean your hair fell out — bald?"

"Totally. Oh, don't look for the wig line, it's grown back since then."

"Why did it fall out?"

Mrs. Miller interrupted to explain. "You see, chemotherapy kills all rapidly dividing cells. That means hair as well as cancer."

Kelly chuckled. "You can't imagine the shock to realize you've answered the door bald as a peeled egg. I think our home teachers passed out!"

"Another time, our physiology class took a field trip to a number of hospitals. In one lab the assistant showed us a dead rabbit and said, 'This rabbit was given adriamycin, a new experimental drug developed for chemotherapy. They're not using it on humans yet.' What does that make me? I didn't know how to say, 'Sorry, sir, you're wrong, I had some last week,' while he was standing there holding a dead rabbit in my face."

"Kelly." Her mother moved closer to us. "I think we're getting away from the subject."

"That's all right," I assured her.

Kelly glanced at her mom, and then at me. "Sorry, Brad. Now what did you want me to tell you about?"

"Commitment." I shuffled to find some clean pages in my notebook. "When did you commit yourself to reaching your goals?"

"I don't remember exactly," she said. "But I remember Dr. Pritchard telling me, 'You might walk again. You might not. It all depends on your determination. It won't come naturally. You will have to make it happen.' And that's what I determined to do. You see, Brad, to continue learning and growing at a rate where I could be happy, I needed to walk."

Sister Miller picked up the conversation. "I think it was only the second day after the operation that they had her working in physical therapy."

Kelly agreed, "Yes, the second day. I guess that's when it happened. That's when I felt an urgent need to commit myself."

Again I marveled at her strength. Here was a girl who was told she might not live to finish her eighth-grade year, yet courageously she commited herself to doing everything she could to graduate from high school and to walk across the stage to receive her diploma. I know this sounds like the story you read in "Faith Promoting Incidents" or heard in family home evening last week. "Beautiful young girl struck down in prime . . . claims she, with Heavenly Father's help, will walk again." Well, that's exactly what it is. But when it happens to someone close to you it isn't remote, as a story is. It's life.

If this period of Kelly's life were made into a movie or a TV special we would now see scenes of Kelly, struggling to overcome the odds, painfully practicing in physical therapy sessions, adjusting to her artificial leg, trying hard not to react to others as they reacted to her leg. We would see flashes of tears and smiles; beautiful photography of a mother and a fourteen-year-old girl struggling to pay the bills, to keep the grades up in school, to reorganize family patterns, to walk again. The program would end with Kelly rising in slow motion from her wheelchair, wind blowing through her hair, to greet a throng of cheering, weeping friends and fans. The whole documentary would take about thirty minutes.

Yet when Kelly did walk across that stage at our high school graduation there were no applauding throngs. The only camera aimed and clicked was her mother's. There was no slow motion, no wind blowing through her hair, no spotlights, no background music. In fact, few people realized that Kelly was walking with the help of an artificial leg. But she knew, and we few knew; and, most important, Heavenly Father knew.

Kelly's story is not an afterschool TV special. It is true. As I write this she is in the middle of the miracle-plus-three-stars stage. She is alive; that says it all. Her remarkable recovery, which is being monitored by doctors and clinics across the nation, has taken much longer than thirty casual TV minutes. Kelly's recovery has taken years. Yet, as she tells me, "When I weigh my experiences, I often find the balance in favor of benefits and blessings which could have come to me in no other way. Every small daily goal has prepared me for more difficult challenges. Every person who encouraged us, Mom and me, expanded our friendships. It has taught me to express love in return."

Now, with an artificial leg, Kelly walks, dances, and rides a bike. She can drive a car and teach tennis, and she wants to learn to ski. It all began when Kelly set a goal and committed herself.

"It's stimulating," she told me. "Commitment to any goal becomes a daily step to high adventure. This is how I can experience heights so exhilaratingly high and lows so devastatingly low that I grow rather than vegetate."

I use this small bit of Kelly's dramatic story to emphasize the power of commitment. I may never be required to face such a traumatic experience, but when I am seeking courage to commit myself to daily goals such as reading scriptures or Church magazines, or calisthenics before bed, I find strength being drawn to me from the experiences of others. My every day does not usually entail earth-shaking situations or life-death decisions. So I look to people who have overcome odds I may never have to face, and I think, "If Kelly can reorganize her whole life to better herself, surely I can read this little article or do these ten pushups to better myself." In my quest to emulate my heroes of the moment I often think, "If they can do it, I can do it."

Kelly's story becomes a symbol of the potential that lies within each of us to change our lives, to master ourselves, to start from where we are, building on the past, as she has, not living in it or forgetting it.

"The business of life is to go forward." That's how Samuel Johnson put it. "Press always forward." That's how my patriarchal blessing puts it. And those are the words that repeated themselves in my mind at the state forensics meet in my junior year.

I was preparing earnestly for a round of competition when Carol, one of my teammates, playfully wound up and accidentally slugged me right in the mouth. We were both surprised. "I'm sorry, it was only a joke," Carol said.

"You know funny jokes," I thought, excusing myself and running to the rest room. Blood was on my suit, my face, all over the sink. "Of all times for this to happen!" I wet a paper towel and began wiping my already egg-size lip. "Why now?" I muttered. "Why now, just before I need to speak at top form?"

My lip was getting larger. I thought about dropping out of the competition and hiding in the bathroom stall; but realistically, I knew that what was done was done. I must begin right there and "press always forward." The paper towels might have been made of sandpaper, they felt so rough. But I managed to stop the blood, said a small prayer, and stalked out of my retreat ready to speak.

That afternoon I overcame a handicap. Nothing to compare with the supreme difficulty Kelly has had to face, of course; but I, like everyone else, deal with problems and frustrations unique to me. Some I can control, some I can't. In that sense our world is made up of handicapped people, each needing to cope and progress; to overcome the opposition we must all face in this life.

It is a well-worn truth that "our differences make the world interesting." If we were all five feet two inches tall, if we all ate pancakes with blueberry syrup, and if we were all equally pessimistic, our world would soon weary of grumpy, five-foot-two-inch pancake-with-blueberry-syrup eaters. It seems to me that it is our differences which add, according to the adage, "the spice of life." How I handle varied interests, thoughts, attitudes, actions, standards, and handicaps enables me to find myself. Will Rogers said it this way: "We are all ignorant; we are just ignorant about different things."

So I live with my handicaps and build on my strengths, with the hope that handicaps might even be turned to strengths — "that every man may improve upon his talent, that every man may gain other talents, yea, even an hundred fold. . . ." (D&C 82:18) I feel that it is our differences, the balance of strengths and weaknesses, that make us each individual, valuable children of a Father in Heaven who loves us, no matter what.

"As I perfect myself eternally, " Kelly told me, "I will

always be setting goals — daily goals, long-range goals, physical, mental, and spiritual goals — and then committing myself with confidence and faith."

The goals Kelly sets are courageous, but what I need to point out too is that for her they are realistic. Too often I get caught up in the flurry of the moment and set outrageous goals without honestly evaluating my experience, interest or capability. It would be foolish for Kelly to set a goal to run in the Olympics and win a gold medal there, because that goal would be unattainable. But for Ezna Schmidt, who lives down the street and runs the mile in four minutes flat, the Olympics would be a realistic goal.

We need lofty goals to furnish incentive, but outrageously high goals, for me at least, serve only to defeat. As Mrs. Miller told me, "Tailor your goals to yourself, then compete with yourself to reach those goals."

"That's what I did," Kelly said. "When I made that commitment to walk, no headlines announced a decision that would change the world, but it changed *my* world. In my mind the growth and happiness that has come periodically over the years since that commitment seem to mound up to a giant ice cream sundae. Finally graduating and walking across that stage was not the cherry to complete my sundae, but only another ingredient added as I keep trying. Do you know what I mean? The ongoing magic in commitment is that I never feel I have reached my goal, whatever it may be, for more than a brief time, before I'm off on my way toward the next one."

"That's why you and I must find happiness and satisfaction in every step along the way, as well as in the achievement itself. Right, Kel?"

As I get swept up in trying, I am continually falling into the pit of postponed happiness. I find myself saying, "I'll be happy when I've lost five pounds," or "I'll be so glad when that due date is past," or "I can hardly wait until I'm finally finished hoeing this garden." But as the weight is lost, I must still be concerned about the problem; as the due date is past, a new deadline looms; and as the last garden row is hoed, new weeds have already begun to show themselves. True, I find satisfaction in reaching any goal, but it is momentary. This is why I must have a good feeling about the process as well as about the product. Too often I've lost the pleasure of the quest in the emphasis on conquest.

It was getting late. I knew it was time to go. Mrs. Miller brought my jacket.

"Well, Kelly." I stood in the open door. With the full moon it hardly seemed dark enough to be ten-thirty. "Do you have any last wise thoughts or sage truths to finish off everything you've taught me?"

Kelly blushed, and stepped out onto the porch with me. "Just that it starts with commitment, Brad. Oh, I realize all that other stuff you tell about in your book is important, but I believe this is what it comes down to — commitment. Every trial you overcome, every hardship you face, and all the work in the world is useless unless you have a goal you're committed to; so when you write your little book, tell 'em that for me. Honest commitment, that's what makes everything fall into place."

Kelly smiled. "Yeah, Brad, you tell 'em that for me."

9

Blister Badges

There is a short stretch of no-name road which exists in defiance of all the "theys" who said it couldn't be done; a symbol of commitment and work. It appears to be an ordinary road, but to our family it is quite extraordinary. If short segments of neighborhood roadways were named, it should be called something impressive like Adamu Avenue. Let me tell you why.

In Ethiopia, while my father was teaching at the Haile Selassie University, my mother also worked there as a secretary. As she tells it, "That's where I came to know Adamu Assegahegn, a personable Ethiopian man whose alert mind and willingness to work made him a large asset to the audiovisual department." I remember Adamu only faintly, for I met him only once. But sometimes I wonder if, as he shook my second-grade hand, he could know what a powerful impact he would have on me. Not right then, but as I grew and as Mom told me the story I shall tell you now.

"I spoke no Amharic," Mom would say, "but Adamu spoke fluent English, then the official second language of Ethiopia. Our friendship expanded as we spoke of rearing families, of world conditions, and of the slow success of recent USAID projects."

"We see the wisdom of what you teach us," Adamu said, "but we are tied by tradition."

As he tried to explain the futile plight of the common man in that ancient Christian empire, Adamu would quote the adage, "When elephants fight, the grass suffers."

"In our country," he would rationalize, "we are learning what we can do, but ordinary people still cannot change things."

Of necessity Adamu kept fit by walking approximately two miles to the University each morning, home for lunch, back again, and finally, home once more in the evening to greet Hannah, his wife, and their seven children. There were times of extreme inconvenience when telephone connections to his part of the city could have saved him the weary walk, but there were no telephones in ordinary homes. He might even have hired a *shashinto* (taxi), but there were no roads to his neighborhood either. The dearth of roadways and telephones, like the ever-present flies, were annoyances which had always existed and over which one had no control. So, although he knew what he could do, Adamu accepted prevailing conditions. It was part of his culture.

Saul, Adamu's eldest son, about nine years old, "was no bigger than our six-year-old," Mother explained. "He had a pair of merry black eyes and an enormous smile, and was such a handsome little fellow it was understandable that his father took great pride in him."

Mom smiled. "Saul and I became friends during his occasional visits to his father's place of work. Through Adamu, Saul would ask, 'Your skin is so white, are you ill?' or 'Where were you taught to pound the typewriter machine?' With Adamu as interpreter, Saul's inquisitive probes and ready wit made him someone special to me.

"Then one frightening night," she continued, "Saul was stricken with such severe abdominal pain that he writhed, clutched his middle, and fell into unconsciousness. How maddening for Adamu, who knew the marvel of modern communication, to be without a telephone! How frustrating to need a taxi and to be without a road!"

In defiance of his superstitious heritage, Adamu wisely chose to take little Saul to the hospital rather than to the witch doctor. He bundled the feverish little body close and began a frantic, stumbling trot over beaten footpaths he knew so well. Clutching Saul, Adamu gasped his way through the dark between swaying eucalyptus trees, around intrusive boulders, all the while cursing the lack of a road which might save his son's life.

Under those adverse conditions, the two-mile run with son held close would be a test of strength for the fittest man. When the doctors told Adamu that Saul's emergency appendectomy was successful and his recovery assured, he collapsed into a nearby chair in relief.

Upon Saul's discharge, a makeshift mattress was laid in the back of our small foreign station wagon. "Saul lay comfortably as I drove him and his parents home from the hospital," Mom remembered. "Of course, the distance by car was minimal, and when we reached the point where the cobbled road ended, Adamu explained, almost apologetically, that they must go the remaining kilometer on foot." Adamu and Hannah arranged the frail Saul high on his father's shoulders and began the jolting march.

Several months went by during which Mom saw the busy Adamu only occasionally, and then only long enough to hear a good report of Saul's return to health. But one morning Adamu burst into Mom's office, laughing and pointing excitedly to blisters on his hands. In a land where the *getauch* (important men) are privileged to be waited upon, and where a person's status is often proved by an inch-long fingernail on the little finger of the left hand (showing he need not do menial labor), blisters are rarely seen. "Yet here was my African friend wearing blisters like badges!" Mom recalled.

Animatedly, he began telling Mom of a most remarkable occurrence. Adamu was the head man of his village-like neighborhood. For years they had needed a road which would allow vehicles access to their inaccessible homes. Appeals for the rent or loan of a bulldozer were lost in a tangle of red tape. Even army colonels and other influential residents of that section of the city could not get action. After that critical night when his child's life was in jeopardy, Adamu had taken his appeal to several different governmental departments. Months passed without response, and his anger mounted proportionately. At last, when the Imperial Highway Authority did respond, the finality of their refusal might have defeated him. Instead, Adamu was spurred to action. He had known what had to be done. Now he was going to do it.

The word was sent forth that Adamu, the mayor, had called a meeting of all citizens of his village. When the questioning crowd assembled he explained their situation, closing with a dramatic challenge.

"There are five hundred people here. That makes a thousand hands!"

A village day was declared. Everyone was to turn out. They would do it! They would build their road by hand!

Adamu admitted to Mom, "I feared the community effort might fail." But later, with touching pride, he told how every man, and his wife and children as well, had come to work on the badly needed road. All day long they dug and grubbed, chopped and hauled, stooped and carried. Even little ones with their *tinnish* (baskets) were kept busy. The day took on a festive quality, with tables of food and boys running along the route supplying goatskins of water for the perspiring workers.

By sundown they stood together to view a roadbed five meters wide and two kilometers long, neatly dug and ready for large cut stones to be fitted later. It was their road, the product of their own hands and backs and sweat.

"I always knew what to do, but nothing got done until I forgot about everyone who told us it was impossible, and simply did it. Now I know," Adamu went on, admiring his own blistered hands, "we can change. It's hard, but we can do it."

It doesn't look like a monument in the conventional sense; but that short road, leading nowhere except to a nondescript African neighborhood, is surely a monument to the power of work and to a dear friend our family will always remember fondly, Adamu.

Usually at this point in Mom's story I find myself cheering the determined hero. "Yea, he did it!" I yell. "He built that road. He overcame the odds. Yea for Adamu!" Then I file Mom's story in the back of my mind until I need a good devotional subject or two-and-a-half-minute talk. But this time I'm challenging myself to file it right up front where I can draw strength from it continually. Even as I write this, I know what I need to do, just as Adamu knew. Now I must follow his example and simply do it; because when the excitement of choosing a goal is over, that's what it comes down to.

As I become more accustomed to my trying steps, they always seem to fall into place when I set a goal. At least, until I get to this step. After I prayed and made the value judgment that writing this book was the best thing for me at the time, I quickly found the right reason and multi-motives. I was thinking positively, so it was easy to commit myself. But when it came down to "applying the seat of your pants to the seat of your chair," as Sinclair Lewis puts it; to rewriting chapters until it hurt; to imposing upon parents and teachers for hours of help; to severely limiting my social life and devoting more than half a year to this goal — yes, when all the excitement and talking stopped and it came down to working, as I knew it must, I needed strength like Adamu's.

That simple stretch of road Mom had told us about so often has become quite real to me. For I, too, am learning how hard it is to ignore all the reasons not to try, and simply to do it.

I remember the day I began writing. I pulled my desk over to the bedroom window so I could gain maximum inspiration from the trees outside. I put some soft music on Dad's stereo to "move" me. Then I sat down and stared at the neatly stacked, terribly blank sheets of paper in front of me. I suppose I expected to drift into a creative dream world and write at least one hundred profound truths before dinner time. After all, isn't that how it happens in the movies? Secretly I think I expected my entire book to come gushing forth from some deep, hidden cavern of my soul and flow onto the paper without a spelling error or crossed-out word.

Since then I have learned that with writing a book like this, as with any worthy goal, inspiration comes from Heavenly Father, and then only if we are prepared to receive it. I could have worked in a root cellar for all the inspiration a scenic view and soft music supplied.

Maybe I should subtitle this chapter "Blood on the Walls," or "You, Too, Can Torture Yourself," for I have never discovered a goal worth working for that doesn't take work. Whether it is daily scripture reading, the graveyard shift that my sister-in-law Moana works as a nurse at the hospital, or the hour a mentally retarded friend spends just tying her shoe, work is hard.

I never really know how to react when people say, "What

fun! You're writing a book!" I guess it is fun, as much fun as work can be. It's not a double-loop-roller-coaster-with-no-hands kind of fun. It's more like what the basketball player experiences who is working like mad to do well in the championship game, jumping, running, dribbling, sweat flowing from every pore on his body. His muscles hurt with every step; his ankles are bandaged; his wrists are bandaged; he's wearing a brace so his bad back won't pop out. Finally, in the last ten seconds of the game he trips over a cheerleader's pompom, crashing to the hardwood floor. The referee accidentally runs over his face totaling two thousand dollars worth of dental work and crushing both contact lenses which had fallen out of his eyes. "How was the game?" his father asked. And what does the basketball player answer? "It was *fun* — really exciting!"

A goal is a goal, and work is work. I haven't found any way around it. But even with sore muscles, the basketball game is fun. Even though it may be my fourth rewrite, the chapter I'm working on is fun. It's hard to explain, but for some reason mowing the lawn is nothing but toil to me. Yet for my brother, who takes pride in our yard and garden, it's fun.

When I was in Toronto, Canada, I met Bryce, an almost-missionary like myself. One day while I was waiting for my ride, Bryce very generously gave me a karate lesson that lasted almost an hour.

"Now, Brad." He came over and slapped me on the back. "If you spend that long every day practicing and stretching out, you'll be ready to take the class when you get home next semester." How could I tell Bryce that I had no lasting interest in karate, no hopes or dreams of becoming a black belt and breaking bricks with bare hands? How could I tell my Canadian friend that I was having problems in fitting all my present interests into school as it was, making an introductory karate class impossible.

For Bryce, karate is important, interesting and fun. He has set goals and spends one hour daily working to achieve his goals. But I have no ambitions in karate right now. To spend my hour a day practicing would not only be a total bore but a misuse of time.

When the work you are doing interests you, or when you

can develop interest in it, then, as tacky as it sounds, that makes work fun. I learned this one day last spring.

"The difference between your brother and you," Maxine said, finishing the conversation we were having about Chris, "is that he really looks good and you, well, Brad, you, ah . . . you look . . . ah. . . ."

I laughed, got out of the car, and waved good-bye. "It's true," I thought as I circled the house to the back door. "Everyone loves Chris's muscles and handsome face, and everyone feels it to be his or her personal responsibility to remind me that my pants are looking too tight." As much as I love Chris, that afternoon I was certain that the biggest, worst problem in the entire world was having an outrageously good-looking, physically fit younger brother.

"Of course he's all that," I thought. "He loves that exercise stuff. I hate running and lifting weights. Well, I'll show them." I headed for the kitchen. "I'll show them what out-of-shape really means."

I was digging diligently through Mom's usual hiding places when at last I felt it taped to the wall behind the dishwasher. A whole package of chocolate chips! Determined to eat the entire thing, tape and all, I began prying my treasure off the wall when the telephone rang. Chris shot in from the other room, answered the phone, and started to take a message.

I dumped my chocolate chips into a bowl and deliberately began downing them by the handful in hopes that he would notice what he had driven me to. But when he hung up he simply started back to his room without a word.

"Chris!" I called. "See what I'm doing?" I was snarfing the chocolate bits so fast I could hardly breathe. "Don't you want to know why?" I choked.

"You're hungry, I guess."

I watched as he turned and disappeared down the hall. Suddenly my plan to become as fat as a house and tell the world it was all his fault seemed as dumb as it actually was. I poured back into the carelessly opened package the chocolate chips that were left, and I was trying to figure a way to tape it behind the dishwasher when Chris came jogging down the hall.

"Have you seen my sweats?"

"Why?" I asked, sucking in my stomach as much as I could.

"I was just going jogging. Want to come?"

With that I gave up on the tape and threw the package dramatically onto the table. "Ugh!" I remarked. "Running is the worst waste of time I've ever heard of."

Chris sat down across the room and started to put on his tennis shoes. "Well, it keeps me in shape."

"So that's the big secret."

"Oh, it's no secret. Everyone knows how good running is." He finished tying his shoes and stood up. "I want to get in shape, so I do it."

"Do it, do it, do it!" I chanted. "You sound like a drill sergeant." I didn't think I wanted to hear what he was about to say, but he said it anyway.

"Everyone knows what to do to be physically fit. I even know people who set goals to get in shape."

(How often I had set that goal for myself!)

"The problem is that they don't do anything about their goals. You can know how good running is for you, but that doesn't mean anything until you do it."

"Yes, sir." I saluted to make sure he knew I had had enough preaching.

I watched as he grabbed his jacket and took off. The half package of chocolate chips settled in my stomach like a glob of cold tar. I finally forced myself to face the truth. Jealousy was the reason I felt Chris was such a problem to me. I wasn't jealous of his body tone, for I knew I too could achieve that. I was jealous of his determination. I knew physical fitness was something I wanted and needed, but I detested exercising so much that I couldn't bring myself to work for it.

"You're not *that* much out of shape," I told myself, flexing before the bathroom mirror. On the other hand, when was the last time I had seen Chris getting winded from just climbing a few flights of stairs. I tugged at the spare tire around my waist. The time had come to finally take control. I really wanted to go through my trying steps. Make the commitment and work. The time had come to forget the excuses and rationalizations I had used all my life and do it.

"I'll start tomorrow morning," I assured myself. "Oh, but there are classes in the morning. So I'll run after school — but then there's rehearsal." Three committee meetings, one interview, and two hours at work later, I dragged into the house, only to remember I'd forgotten my neighbor's wedding reception. "I can't run now," I argued, as I got home at 11:30 p.m. "This isn't fair. No wonder Chris can stay fit. He has time to work out."

"We are not endeavoring to get ahead of others, but to surpass ourselves." Elder Hugh B. Brown's statement memorized some time before in seminary hit me like a running shoe at the side of my head.

Sure I was busy. I had a lot of responsibilities that ate up my time, but right alongside those disadvantages were my advantages, and I was overlooking them. After all, how many other high school kids had access to the university track and showers? And since the field house was so close, I could just walk to school after running in the mornings.

The following day I woke early, as planned, and ran three miles; then I surprised myself by meeting all my responsibilities for the day. I woke up the next morning with legs so unbearably sore that I almost needed a wheelchair just to get to the breakfast table. All I could manage was to chug a half-mile around the track and then limp through the rest of the day. When I finally hobbled home I collapsed on the family room rug where Chris was reading.

"I hate running," I moaned. "Anyway, I'm too tired to run tomorrow morning. I can't move, and I haven't lost one single pound."

Chris didn't say anything, but I was reading his mind. "Don't give me a listing of reasons why you don't run. Everyone has excuses. It's performance that counts." Chris shut the magazine and chucked it on the table next to him.

"You can't give up now, Brad," he said. "You've already committed yourself." I knew he was right.

Slowly and painfully over the next few weeks I began to change my attitude. "Dad's been jogging for years and he loves it," I reasoned. So I endured and plugged ahead with faith that running around that unwelcoming track for a half-hour every morning would get me where I wanted to be. I have to admit I hated every step at first, but now that I've been running for several months, sure enough, in a weird way I do enjoy it. Physical fitness is a long-range goal I'll be working at for the rest of my life because it's important to me now. That's why I'm enjoying it, because I used self-discipline. I forced myself to be interested in something important.

I reminded myself that

> The heights by great men reached and kept,
> Were not attained by sudden flight;
> But they, while their companions slept,
> Were toiling upwards in the night.
>
> —Longfellow

I still have a long way to go before I even begin to resemble Chris. But I'm working, I'm trying.

10

Why Train Under a Fool?

"Oh, Brad, look at this. Isn't it just the absolute?" Peggy, a girl in my ninth-grade art class slunk up to me, popping her gum obnoxiously close to my face.

"I've drawn this wild picture. It took me almost all period, but it was worth it. Don't you just love it?"

I stared at the paper placed on the table before me. "I didn't know I was so talented," Peggy went on, "but now I've decided to draw for a career. How much do you think I could sell this one for — considering it's my first picture, of course."

"Yeah, I guess you will have to sell this one cheap."

"Cheap?" she bellowed. "Someday this will be a collector's item!"

I restudied the picture. What could I say? Any of the second graders in my Mom's classroom could have done a more professional job.

Peggy cleared her throat. "I've tried to make it realistic. I wanted it to look kinda like I took it with my camera. Did you notice the cute little dog under the bridge on this side?"

I'm glad she told me it was a dog. It looked more like a sick muskrat. I asked, "Why don't you show it to Mrs. Houghton? She might tell you how to make it look better."

"Oh, yes!" Peggy squealed. "She's so smart, and such a good drawer. I can't wait to show her my dog. That's the best part." She flashed me a cheesecake grin and skipped off to the front of the room.

Within moments she came back storming. "That dumb Mrs. Houghton. She doesn't know anything!"

I don't think I really understood Peggy's frustration. Mrs. Houghton had always helped me with my art projects.

In fact, as I look back at everything I've done and realize that I've never been entirely on my own, it's humbling. Occasionally I think back as far as I can, trying to remember one worthwhile thing I have tried and accomplished by myself. I haven't found one yet. So far my life has been completely surrounded by outstanding parents, friends, teachers, coaches — all lifting me, all influencing me for good. Whenever I'm trying, I'm never alone, at least I shouldn't be, for as Og Mandino and Buddy Kaye write in *The Gift of Acabar*, "He who teaches himself has a fool for a master." The way I figure it, with so many specialized instructors and counselors willing to help me develop myself to better serve others, why go it alone? Why train under a fool?

Peggy shoved her picture at me again and continued complaining. "Mrs. Houghton says it's a good beginning! How do you like that!"

"And . . . what else did she say?" I prodded.

"That's it! Good for a start. Can't she see it's finished? I just wanted her to tell me where I could sell it, and all she says is, 'It needs more work!' Now, I ask you, isn't that dumb? Waste time working on this picture when I could be drawing another to sell!"

"But you only spent the last forty-five minutes on it," I offered weakly.

"That's what Mrs. Houghton said." Peggy knotted her face into a pinched ball and mimicked, "You can't expect perfection the first time. These dumb teachers!" She patted the tight curls around her face. "They're trying to stifle my creativity. Well, I won't let them," she went on. "I don't need anyone's help."

"Are you kidding? Nobody can learn all about drawing by himself." Just then the bell rang, saving me from getting in any deeper.

For Peggy to reach her newly set goal to become a professional artist, if it were something she really wanted, would take practice and training from skilled instructors. She needed classes from knowledgeable artists, but in her mind apparently she had determined that no one was qualified to train her supernatural talent. Disregarding advice and lessons from Mrs. Houghton, Peggy had decided to work all by herself. To do the work was a wise decision, but to choose herself as teacher was foolish. Trying and reaching goals doesn't have to be a me-against-the-world undertaking.

As the class ended I slid my picture inside my health book and headed into the narrow hallway. Peggy tailed me. I was getting a little tired of the whole thing, until I turned and saw her eyes. Other kids shoved past us, so we dodged to a place against the wall.

"Brad," Peggy said. There was a long pause. "It isn't easy when somebody, I mean. . . ." I watched the tears forming. ". . . When somebody says that what you've done isn't . . . ah, . . . perfect." She looked down at the picture in her hand. Well, what I mean is, when they think it's . . . ah . . ." Her voice had melted into a broken whisper. ". . . When they think it's rotten."

"No," I replied softly. "It isn't easy."

"Well, . . ." She took a deep breath, flushing with embarrassment at the seriousness of the conversation. "I know I could learn to draw like Mrs. Houghton wants, but it's so much work!" She stepped backward into the nearly empty hall and forced a smile. "I'd rather be a doctor or a model anyway." She juggled her books to an upright position, popped her gum as though nothing had happened, and nodded, "See ya, Brad."

The tardy bell rang. I watched Peggy disappear around the corner. She moved away a few months later, and I haven't heard of her since. Sometimes I wonder if she still aims to be a doctor or a model, artist or airplane pilot, or any of the other fifty careers she spoke about. Whatever she plans to do, one thing is certain: if she's really putting her plan into practice, somewhere between that ninth-grade art class and now she had to learn the same thing I'm still trying to learn — the art of being teachable.

We are told in the scriptures to humble ourselves, become as little children, and remain teachable. For me, it has never been as easy as it sounds to totally trust others as they train me. I know it's important, but how can I remain teachable?

As often as I ask that question, I never hear anything new. The scriptures give age-old answers. Prophets repeat the same theme. I know what I need to do. As with any facet of self-improvement; it's just a matter of doing it.

As I sat in the dentist's chair, covered with cloths and clamps, I almost used my free agency to reject what I knew would help me. I could have said, "Dr. Morton is not going to touch my wisdom teeth." And when he came toward my mouth with that shot needle, I could have said, "No way, doctor or not; he doesn't know anything." But inside I knew he was qualified, and I knew the operation had to be done for my best good. Sometimes it hurts to let others help, but it would be a long climb up the mountain to perfection alone. If we're here to help each other, then why train under a fool?

Of course, my oldest brother, Wayne, reminds me that if I do nothing but take, the scale is upset; and the balance which must be kept in life is lost. Likewise, it is upset if I do nothing but give. You help me, I'll help you. Learn from my mistakes, and I'll learn from yours. Build on my strengths, and I'll build on yours. That's working together, and that's how we'll make it.

11

Martha, What Happened To Your Hair?

Automatically my hand traced the deep scratches on my desk top. It was just something I always did when there was nothing else to do. Miss Catlin continued passing out the clean, sealed envelopes. "Stevenson, Taylor...."

I already knew what the letters said. Everyone did. We had received one the previous year, too, when we were advanced to the fourth grade. "Congratulations," I remembered. "We are pleased to inform you that your child has passed all the requirements for advancement...."

"Wilcox." Miss Catlin stepped toward my desk and handed me my envelope. She smiled. We both knew that my letter didn't say that this year. Ever since our family had returned from Ethiopia, Dad and Mom had talked about keeping me back to join my own age group.

"You started school a year early," Dad explained, "because there was no kindergarten. We're trying to fix that now and do what's best for you."

It didn't matter that much to me. Most of my friends were in third grade anyway. In fact, as I sat waiting for the final bell of the school year I even felt a little tinge of superiority. "Next year," I thought, "I'll know all the answers, just as Brian did this year."

As I dashed for the door, Miss Catlin stopped me. Usually I wouldn't have minded, because I loved to be with her. I always bragged about having the prettiest teacher in the school, but today I was in a hurry. "When we talked the other day," she said, "you said you felt good about it. Do you still feel good, Brad?"

"Sure, or else I wouldn't stay in fourth grade again." The other kids had all passed me, and now I was alone with Miss Catlin. "I gotta go, or Brian and Dave will walk home without me."

She laughed and followed me into the hall. "I'm glad you're still feeling good, because this is the best thing for you. When you're my age you'll look back and be glad we've made this choice."

"Yeah," I called back, not really listening.

"It might be hard sometimes, Brad, but it's the right thing."

"See ya, Miss Catlin. See you next year." What would be so hard about staying in fourth grade, anyway?

I had to run to catch up to Brian and Dave, who had left the grounds and were already halfway through the orchard toward home. Brian had opened his letter and was opening Dave's when I finally caught up.

"Don't," Dave said. "Miss Catlin told us not to open them until we got home."

Brian stopped and looked up. "Don't you want to know if you passed?"

"You bet I do."

"Then open the letter," Brian urged. "They all say the same thing."

Dave took the envelope and finished lifting the ragged flap. Brian grabbed my envelope. I snatched it back. "Aren't you going to open it?" he asked.

Just then Dave shoved his letter between us. "I passed!" he declared triumphantly.

Brian began walking again. "Everyone does," he stated knowledgeably. "Even Terri, and she can't even do times tables."

To me, Brian seemed to be the one person on earth who knew everything. He even knew the Articles of Faith and every President of the Church and of the United States. I liked Brian, but today he was bothering me.

"Well," he glared, "aren't you going to find out if you passed?"

"Uh, uh." I kept walking toward the road. "I'm going to wait till I get home."

"What's the matter?" Dave said. "Don't be scared. They pass everybody. It's a law, I think."

Suddenly Brian grabbed my letter and began to open it. "Give me that!" I started to chase him. "I don't want to open it yet!"

We scurried around several trees, just long enough for Brian to tear open the envelope and read the first line of my letter. I just missed snatching it from him when he yelled, "Hey, Dave, Brad's is different." I tackled him in the thick grass.

"Give it!" I yelled.

"You didn't pass!" Brian was shocked.

"He didn't?" Dave ran toward us.

I stood up and attempted to fold the wrinkled paper back into the envelope. "You didn't pass!" Brian started to laugh. "You're a dummy. Only dummies get held back."

Dave ran up next to me. "Are you kidding? Didn't you really pass?"

I didn't answer, because I was fighting the tears. "You must be retarded," Brian yelled. "You're even dumber than Terri."

"I am not! I just started school too young."

"You're stupid!"

"I am not!" I slugged his stomach as hard as I could. He swung a fist and clobbered me in the side of the head, knocking me off balance. For an instant I didn't know where I was. I squirmed in the tall grass. My ear was ringing wildly. Brian jumped and landed on my side. I couldn't see through my tears; I just kept swinging as hard as I could. There was a taste of blood but I didn't know where it was coming from.

Every fight I'd ever had before had been with brothers, and that was usually for fun. But this was different. No one was kidding. I wanted to hurt him. We bumbled through the grass, punching aimlessly, until he bit me. He grabbed my arm and bit me!

Pain sizzled. Fury flooded through me. Like the bite of a

mad dog his teeth remained clamped on my arm, though I screamed and kicked. Finally Dave hit him square on the back, and Brian let go.

"Knock it off!" Dave shoved us apart. "Come on, let's go home."

Brian stood up, and Dave dragged him toward the road. "You just wait, stupid," Brian yelled back. "I'll tell everyone how dumb you are."

I didn't move. My arm felt paralyzed. Tears ran sideways across my bloody nose and dropped into the weeds beneath me. Actually it was only a few minutes but it seemed like an hour that I lay there whimpering in self-pity. Finally I straightened my shirt where the buttons were ripped off and stood up. "I'm *not* dumb." I picked up the rumpled envelope. "I'm *not* dumb!" I repeated with vehemence.

I think that was the first conscious self-evaluation I ever made. Amazingly enough, I knew that it was Brian who was acting dumb. I was smart to be staying in fourth grade; and, despite bruises and blood, that decision still felt good. Suddenly I understood what Miss Catlin meant when she said it might be hard sometimes. But, hard or not, it was still the right thing.

This is the last step in my "trying" checklist; this is where I review, reevaluate and check up on myself.

"Tell us about your Church." Eight other people had crammed into a train compartment that should have seated only six. All were staring questioningly at us. They couldn't have asked three more eager sixteen-year-old missionaries. Laura Wilkinson, Steve Perry, and I all began to talk at once. The overcrowded train jerked forward and began to chug slowly out of the station at Geneva, Switzerland. It was 1976, America's bicentennial year, and we were three of only a handful of Mormons in our All-American touring choir of three hundred. I think most of the group knew we were LDS; but until then no one had shown any particular interest. Suddenly, here were eight red-white-and-blue uniformed bodies awaiting our pronouncements. There were five different religions represented among us, but it was the Mormons everyone wanted to know more about.

The train picked up speed as we traveled farther into the storied countryside. My dad had given me a mountain of pamphlets "just in case" moments like this came up, but I had carefully packed them where they wouldn't take up much space — right on top of my Book of Mormon, which was now under three hundred other suitcases in the baggage car. It was my big chance to introduce the gospel, and I had nothing but myself and a mindful of half-memorized seminary scriptures back there in the cobwebs of my memory.

As the train wound its way through the posteresque countryside, I felt as though we were viewing the first scene of *The Sound of Music* over and over. By noon, Laura, Steve and I had touched on almost all of what seemed to our listeners to be our strange Mormon beliefs. One girl, Gwen, couldn't get over the fact that Mormons don't drink coffee.

"I knew you guys didn't smoke, but no coffee! How do you live?"

Even after three hours in that stuffy train compartment everyone was still so involved in questions and answers that the three of us took turns in eating when the box lunches were delivered. Hot as it was, and cramped as it was, I found myself enjoying this chance to explain my beliefs. It was almost like a seminary game.

"Gwen, we don't drink coffee because the Lord has commanded us not to in the Word of Wisdom," I explained. "Coffee contains caffeine." Gwen seemed lost. "The word of what?" Steve went on and explained it along with the harms of caffeine, while I began downing the dry half-chicken lunch.

"You kids live a deprived life," Gwen laughed.

I just smiled and fumbled through some salty potato chips and tired carrot sticks. My mouth was dry. I felt far beyond thirsty. Finally the drinks were served. Wouldn't you know it? Coke! Ice cold, wet cans of Coca Cola!

I looked out of the train window nervously. We were passing though the green wet hills of northern France, but my throat felt as if we were lost in the middle of the Mojave Desert. I was going to refuse the cold, moist can — I really was. But when I opened my mouth, all that came out was potato chips. A few drops of condensation trickled onto my hand. I closed my eyes and imagined the glorious liquid coolness that could so easily be soothing my throat. I thought of the stinging carbonation numbing my tongue and tingling behind my nose.

I was trying to be a good example. I had committed myself to being a missionary. But now, with half a wrinkled chicken in my stomach, was it worth it?

Reluctantly I reached to give my can away. "Wait," I told myself. "I've held this for more than a minute and no one has mentioned that Coke has caffeine. What luck! Gwen must not know. I can drink it and. . . ."

"Would anyone like my drink?" Laura asked. "Coke contains caffeine, so I won't be drinking it."

Gwen was alarmed. "You mean Coke is against your Word of Wisdom, too?"

"Not exactly," Steve said. "It's a personal decision, but our Church leaders have counseled us against drinking any caffeinated drinks."

The whole group stared at the can in my lap. With my finger already under the tab lid, I had to check up fast. "Now, Brad," I told myself, "here's what you can do. Tell Gwen your Coke is different, a special kind, or sneak down the hall to the W.C. and drink it there, or say 'Ha, ha, fooled you! — I'm not a Mormon after all,' and drink the Coke that is tempting you so much."

My goal to be a good example and a missionary was great before I ate lunch, but now was it still important enough to suffer these pangs of dehydration for?

"Here, Gwen." I stretched out my arm. "You look thirsty enough for a double."

Before my life is over, I'm sure, I'll ride many trains and come across many Gwens. I'm sure that hot European day was not the last time I'll have to reevaluate my goals in the face of discomfort or even hardship. My priorities and attitudes might change somewhat as I grow, so to insure that my life can continue to grow for the better I'll always have to check up.

I remember that when I was little I always wanted to be a teacher — until one day I saw a fireman-hero movie and decided that being a fireman was my role in life; at least until the next basketball game, when I determined to be a professional ball player. Next it was an astronaut, then a doctor, and then a movie actor. As hard as I worked at my dream of the moment, after a period I'd discover it wasn't something I wanted anymore. Who knows? My long-range career goals at present could completely change after my mission, or maybe they'll just expand. I suppose, whether it was in fourth grade, Europe, or any other time, it always seems to come down to this: as Brad Wilcox climbs his mountain to perfection, check-ups are mandatory. Have I prayed and made my value judgment? Am I doing the right thing? Am I self-motivated with the right reasons and multi-motives? Am I maintaining a positive attitude? Am I acting and not reacting? Do I have the faith to commit myself and work?

Checkups give me the chance to go through my other trying steps and honestly evaluate.

As with any effort, there are times in goal-jumping when I am just kidding myself and I know it. When I stopped planting my personal rows in our family garden I checked up and told myself that my interests had matured, whereas the honest reason was that I resented the extra work. When I quit taking piano lessons in seventh grade, I checked up and told myself that taking those lessons wasn't something I wanted to do anymore; but actually, I was just afraid of what a few kids might think if they found out I liked music.

I've abandoned too many goals when the work was hard and the end was out of sight, on the rationalization that they didn't fit anymore. I'd tell myself I had checked up when in reality I had given up.

It was my junior year in high school, and our music department was putting on Gilbert and Sullivan's *The Mikado*. I was cast as Nanki Poo, the son of Japan's emperor, who flees his father's court rather than marry Katisha, an older woman with "a caricature of a face."

That's when I met Martha West. I couldn't understand why Mr. Barker cast such a pretty girl to play that hideously ugly, bloodthirsty character — at least, not until the night of dress rehearsal. I had stayed late at school, finishing what was meant to be a Japanese bridge. By the time I went home, showered, gathered up my costumes, and returned to school the dress rehearsal had already begun.

"Brad, you're on! That's your cue." Without noticing who

was pushing me toward the stage, I stumbled across my masterpiece of a bridge and gasped my first line.

During some of the upcoming scenes, I managed to throw on enough makeup to pass as a Japanese minstrel. When the time came for Katisha's entrance I was positioned on the front of the stage, as we had rehearsed. With total gusto I sang the cue, and Martha strode over the bridge.

When I turned and saw her in full costume and makeup, I fell right off the front of the stage. I was floored (literally!). Never had I seen such grotesque hair. Martha's long, shining brown hair was sprayed black and ratted into an enormous bun full of chopsticks, Japanese lanterns, and even birds. The whole mess stuck out a couple of feet on all sides of her head.

In spite of my laughter I was able to crawl back on stage. I tried to finish the play but I couldn't. Every time I had to look at that bushel-basket size hairdo on formerly pretty Martha, I had to laugh.

"The hair is a masterpiece, but why did you do it?" I asked her after the rehearsal.

"Isn't it great?" She punched the ratted glob from here to there before the dressing-room mirror.

"I love it," I laughed. "But why?"

"Anybody could play Katisha, but I want my character to be the ugliest and oldest and most memorable of all Katishas. Last week I was looking through a book of Mr. Barker's, and I saw a picture like this. Isn't it a scream?"

"It's perfect." That's all I could say. "Everyone will love it."

"They'd better. It cost me thirty-five dollars, and I'll have to sleep on a brick for the rest of the week."

"You mean it's permanent?" I asked.

"Until I wash it, it is."

I folded the last of my costume and began bouncing cotton balls off the hair next to me. "How do you get through doors?" I joked.

"Doors aren't a problem yet, but it's a pain to drive. I have to sit so low I can hardly see the road."

A few more people left, making us the last ones there. "Well, Martha," I began to turn out the lights. "It will make the whole play."

She giggled. "I know. I can't wait for tomorrow night." Martha picked up her costume bag, and I switched out the light. All at once she screamed. I fumbled for the switch. She screamed again.

"What's wrong?" I yelled. Thc lights went on. Martha rushed to the mirror. "What's the matter?" I asked again.

"Oh, what have I done?" she half-screamed, half-moaned. "I have to come to school tomorrow!"

I promised to wait outside at seminary so she wouldn't have to walk in alone. When Martha finally arrived I couldn't decide if she looked so white because she was scared, or just because the hair was sprayed so black.

"Good morning," I smiled. She lifted one eyebrow and glared at me.

I opened the door wide, and Martha swept regally into the room. The entire class gasped, I think one girl almost fell off her chair, but I couldn't be sure because I was walking behind the hair. When the bell rang, poor Martha didn't move.

"Come on," I said, "you don't want to walk into English last today."

"I'm not moving," she mumbled. "Did you hear them laughing at me?"

"They all know you're in the play, Martha," I coaxed. "You can't miss a whole week of school just because your hair looks like an atom bomb."

"You're a big help." We left the building. When we got to the back door of the school, I think I was feeling as hesitant as Martha.

"I don't think I can go through with it." She froze.

"Look, you're the one who wanted to look ugly, and it cost thirty-five dollars." I think it was the wrong thing to say, but it got her through the door.

As we marched down main hall, people shoved their way to either side, leaving the entire center of the hallway for Martha. Everyone stared. A few pointed. Some laughed right out loud. "I feel like a leper," Martha whispered out of the side of her mouth."

"Unclean, unclean," I chanted.

"Really funny, Brad," but it was the first smile she had given all morning.

By noon, the gigantic mountain of hair had become the

talk of the school. Everyone wanted to find Martha and see if it was as unbelievable as rumor had it. Martha even had a small cult of sophomores who waited outside her classes and followed in awed astonishment as she made her way to her locker.

"I felt like a circus sideshow freak," she told me as I drove her home.

"That's only because you look like a circus sideshow freak." I was trying to cheer her up, but she just looked at me.

I asked, "I guess you've already heard all the Halloween's-over jokes by now, haven't you?" She nodded. "Well, get excited, Martha. It's opening night."

That evening my excitement mounted as Katisha's entrance grew closer. Finally, I positioned myself on the front of the stage and sang, "Ah, 'tis Katisha, the maid of whom I told you." Martha swished across the bridge and the audience went wild.

They say that in Shakespeare's time, if the "groundlings" (patrons who sat on the ground of the Globe Theatre to watch the plays) saw something they liked they would throw dirt in the air, stamp, scream, yell and rip their clothing. When Martha West came on the stage that night, we had nearly the same thing happen in our high school auditorium.

When Martha took her bow in the curtain call she was met with a thunderous standing ovation. "It's worth it," she exclaimed. "I've thought about it, and the hair is worth it."

But at noon the next day, as I picked out spit wads, gum and pencils from deep inside the tangled mass, she whimpered, "It's not worth it. How can I last through a whole week?"

Martha slumped forward in her chair and looked around the empty conference room. "I don't know, Brad," she said. "I thought I was doing the right thing when I got my hair all ratted up, but now I just don't think it's worth it."

"What about last night and how you felt then?" I reminded.

"The Junior Prom is coming up, and no one will ever ask me like this."

I stood back and surveyed the hair to make sure it was cleaned out and ready for the eyes of the world again.

"Oh, I know I said that developing my talents and this

character and all was important, but I just don't know how important." The bell rang. She rose stiffly and gathered her books. Without even looking back she walked to the door. "I guess I just want to wash this dumb hair and get asked to the prom." Martha sighed heavily, opened the door sufficiently to pass through, and disappeared into the hall. I stood alone for another minute in the conference room.

"She's checking up," I thought. "Martha's been evaluating this situation ever since dress rehearsal, and I haven't even realized it." I wished there were a way I could help, but I knew from experience that a self-evaluation can only be done by yourself.

I glanced at the wall clock. It was time to get going. I couldn't say whether the goal she set was still worth reaching, because only Martha knew herself well enough to honestly make that decision. I walked to my locker and fumbled with the combination.

"Let's get to class, people. Let's move it."

Ordinarily Mr. Lindstrom would have interrupted my chain of thought, but not today. "Whatever she decides — to keep her hair or not — I hope she's checking up and not giving up." I turned the corner toward C wing. "That's the difference between self-improvement and self-degradation." I barely beat the bell into my next class.

"Now that thought was profound," I decided smugly. "I think I'll letter it on a sign and post it in Martha's hair."

12

Chapter One - Part Two

Flames jumped and snapped as the log crumbled into embers. Pulsating coals separated and fumed like angry lovers. I shifted on the warm couch and pulled Grandma's soft quilt close around my chin. Skinny shadows skipped across the dark ceiling.

Outside, the unexpected snow kept falling. Heavy flakes pawed at the dining room window as though silently begging for the warmth of my fire. I should have been concerned. I didn't know how long the storm would last.

"What if they close the road at Point of the Mountain?" I thought. "Then Mom and Dad couldn't get home until tomorrow. Well, anyway, they're safe." I leaned my head back and smiled. This was what I'd been waiting for; an evening with nothing to do but write.

I settled myself to enjoy the privacy and the fire. I hadn't spent time completely by myself since way back before Christmas, so it felt good to be alone.

Sometimes, when I get caught up in the pressure of this hurried world, I think heaven will be right on our family room couch, feeling the warmth of our home, watching the snow outside, pulling Grandma's quilt safely around my shoulders and drinking a second cup of Postum.

When the fire at last began to die, I decided that was my signal to get back to work on the book. I forced myself to stand up, tossed a small log from the woodpile into the weak flames, and hurried into the bedroom. Even in my flannel shirt, the house was a little cold without the comfort of my quilt. I grabbed some folders and my notebook and then ran back to the couch.

I recalled that when I was a small boy and the house was dark like this, I used to imagine there were alligators under the couch. If I didn't jump high and fast — snap! Off would come my feet! I could remember hesitating to kneel down some nights at family prayer because of the slimy creatures I was almost certain were lurking under the couch waiting to bite my bare toes. Now I laughed at myself to think that I would be going on a mission in only months, and yet I still leaped to the couch to fool the alligators.

I propped pillows behind my head and wrestled with the quilt. Then, with my writing journal spread across my lap, I stopped noticing the snow and the late hour. Slowly I lost myself in trying to strengthen a weak outline for chapter 12. I'd been struggling with that chapter for quite a while, but I kept hitting dead ends that forced me back to the writing journal (a junk place for any quotes that have impressed me, or for strange characters who might one day find their way into a short story). This scrap pile of ideas is a last resort when I have no lightbulbs flashing in my head. Usually a skim through the old journal would revitalize my brain, but tonight even that wasn't working.

Standing up, I leaned to pile what was left of the wood onto the dwindling fire which, like chapter 12, was turning to ashes. I was feeling frustrated.

"Why isn't it working?" I questioned. "Here is the night I've dreamed of; I'm completely alone with nothing to do but write, and I have nothing to write."

I flipped open the journal again and sifted through the last few quotations: "I shall allow no man to belittle my soul by making me hate him" — Booker T. Washington. That one was scrawled on a table napkin from last year's youth conference. And Nathan Hale's "I regret that I have but one life. . . ." was scratched on a torn sheet of notebook paper.

"Maybe I don't need a chapter 12." I shifted on my pillows. "I've explained all the steps. What else do I have to say?" All along I had pictured chapter 12 as a tight little conclusion that would tie it all together. But I had worked for weeks now, with nothing but eighty-five overused quotes in my junk journal.

I was at this point when I pulled out a light blue piece of paper. I remembered Mom handing it to me after some Relief Society meeting, but I'd stuffed it away without even reading it. This is what was on it:

> *It costs so much to be a full human being that there are very few who have the enlightenment or the courage to pay the price. . . . One has to . . . reach out to the risk of living with both arms. One has to embrace the world like a lover.*
>
> —Morris L. West
> *The Shoes of the Fisherman*

"That's powerful," I said to myself. "It says it all. I think I'll just tack it on the end of chapter 11 and call the book finished." With that decision I shoved the whole scribbled mess out of sight under the couch. "Food for the alligators" I thought, as I snuggled down to enjoy the last few moments of firelight.

The next Tuesday, Wednesday and Thursday were the busiest days I can remember. I think I rewrote everything three times, and chapter 11 at least six.

"That quotation just doesn't fit," I reasoned. But even though it seemed out of place, it was the closest thing to a powerful ending I could come up with, so it stayed.

My schoolwork was piling up. Two tests were looming at the end of the month. The snow, beautiful and refreshing earlier, had half-melted into dingy, sticky slush that only slowed me down. It was still snowing on Friday. That afternoon I arrived at my voice class early for the first time. Class began with the usual "Everyone in this group needs to be more dedicated" lecture, but it was interrupted when the door opened.

"Sorry I'm late." Kim quickly took a seat across the room from me. I caught her eye and pulled some sort of face in greeting.

I had met Kim Woolf during our junior year in high

school. I sat through entire classes, as I was doing just then, wondering what made one girl so beautiful inside and out. All I could do was smile when she turned and found me staring at her. She smiled back. Her deep brown eyes made me feel like a wax candle under a sunlamp.

Our instructor, who was sitting at a piano in the center of the room, began playing some warm-ups. Above his head I caught the "thumbs up" signal Kim was sending. She was finished! She was actually finished reading my entire manuscript! Suddenly I was embarrassed. Kim was the first person to read what I had written — my thoughts, my words. Had I said everything I needed to? Had I said it right?

I can't remember whether I was singing or not, but if I had been I wasn't anymore. Only the night before I had given Kim the eleven-chapter manuscript because I needed her reaction.

I looked up at the clock above the door. Still forty-five minutes of class left before I'd be able to talk with Kim! I felt like a father whose wife was having a baby — but then, I don't know how that feels yet. Instead, I'll say I felt as I did during the last ten seconds of our basketball game when my high school was one point behind. Those ten seconds had seemed like forty-five minutes; and these present forty-five minutes seemed endless.

"I just finished it, Brad, just before I came to class. That's why I was late." Kim rushed to me through the mass of students heading for the door. I searched her face for early signs of her reaction.

"I'm not a pro when it comes to books," she went on. "I mean, like this Mr. Bickerstaff you talk about. But I like it. I really like your book."

I hugged her. "That's why I asked you to read it first."

While we talked I led Kim out of the classroom and toward the stairs. She handed me the bulky manilla envelope. "I hope it has a nicer cover than that when it's printed," she laughed. "Do you have a title yet?"

"Mr. Bickerstaff said we worry about that a little later. Why, do you have any ideas?"

Because the railing had just been painted, Kim was taking careful steps down the twisty staircase. "Well, since you've asked, I just happen to have come up with the perfect one. How about *Fish Heads and Rice*?"

"What does that have to do with anything?"

"Nothing, but it will make people curious enough to pick it up."

We were nearly at the door. "Maybe we should just call it the Baruba Book," I said.

In the end, as you see, we called it something like that. Having read the book, you will realize that the word *success* in the title doesn't have the meaning of excelling, winning, being on top, as so often it does in modern books. You know I'm talking about trying, about each of us putting out the effort to develop his own life and talents. To me, that's success. It doesn't matter how clever other people may be, or seem to be, how much they achieve in chosen fields. (Remember, no one has it all — you may well be superior in important characteristics to many of the great achievers.) You, I, everyone — each of us is a personal success if we set good and realistic goals and achieve them, progressively increasing the difficulty of our goals. And if we do this, whether we receive any acclaim from the world or not makes no difference — we are indeed a success.

But Kim and I didn't know then what the book would be called. I leaned hard to open the glass door against the storm. We skidded across the parking lot to my old heap of a Chevy. Thick snowflakes covered us like cake frosting. The right door was jammed as usual, so without fighting further I hurried Kim to my side of the cold car.

"Thanks for the ride home," she said.

I didn't even bother to say it was my pleasure, because she already knew that. I brushed what seemed like a two-ton glacier off my head and coat and began fumbling with my key chain.

"Tell me again, Kim." I shifted to reverse and sloshed out of the parking lot.

"Okay, Mr. Ego, I liked it. I like all of chapter one; the part about the English test and then Ethiopia. But oh, one thing that did kind of bother me . . . when you're talking to that guy, you know, the dropout — you never say his name."

"I know."

"But don't you think people will want to know?"

"He was my friend, Kim, and that's all that's important."

"I guess you're right," she agreed.

A traffic light turned yellow. I tried to speed up and to get through the intersection, but with all the snow on the roads my acceleration hardly made any difference.

Kim went on: "I remember who he was. I never really did know him well. It was always just 'Hi' in the hall. You weren't the only one who was surprised when he dropped out, though. Everyone in the orchestra was surprised. He even had a solo number."

She turned sideways on the seat to face me. "Where is he now?"

"I don't know. I think he moved to Arizona for a while, and then someone said he was working in Illinois back where my grandpa lives in Aurora; but Maria Covey just told me he's moved again."

Kim's voice was soft. "Do you think we'll ever see him again?"

"I don't know that either." I slouched down a little to see more clearly past the struggling windshield wipers.

"Now that you've written a whole book telling him how to try, I think it would be kind of fun to meet him downtown someday." She laughed. "I can just see you running up to him and saying, 'Here's the book that will change your life in fifteen minutes!' If you saw him again, what would you say, Brad?"

"Not that, for sure!"

Kim continued more thoughtfully: "He wouldn't even remember me, but if I saw him in the Mall someday I'd yell, 'Have I got a book for you!' I'd love to see the look on his face if I marched up to him and said, 'Here's the book that will tell you how to try.' "

"But, Kim," I said, as I turned up the dead-end road to her house, "he never asked how. He asked why."

She studied my face. "Why what?"

I paused for a moment as I remembered. "He asked, 'Why try?' He was saying, 'After everything is said and done and you know all the how-to's, why try?' "

This time it was Kim who paused. "What did you answer?"

I slipped somewhat sideways to a stop in her driveway. "You know, Kim, that's what's been bothering me. I don't think I did answer him."

Then, as we sat in the early evening, something happened. For some reason, suddenly all I cared about was to be able to honestly answer that question. Why try? All at once those two words became supremely important. There had to be an answer and I had to find it, otherwise my steps were worthless, my book was worthless, and everything I was living for was all worthless.

"Kim, I remember he told me that trying is like making your bed. Why do it every morning if you're just going to sleep in it again? What should I have responded when he said, 'I'll keep living even if I don't try. I'll wake up tomorrow even if I drop out today, and I'll. . . .'

"I interrupted him, 'But will you be happy? Will you be fulfilled? Will you be the person you want to be?' I remember him staring into the rain. Then he said, 'I guess not, but will you?' "

After a moment Kim urged, "What did you say next?"

"I said something like, 'Yes, I will be happy when I do it right. I will be fulfilled.' Then he exploded angrily, 'And I guess you'll hike right up that dumb mountain and become perfect too, won't you?'

"It's been a year, but I'll never forget the fury in his face. His eyes mocked me as he said, 'And Brad Wilcox's not-one-cavity-smile, high-school-graduate life will go down in history as. . . .' He didn't finish."

I sought Kim's eyes. "I'm kind of glad he didn't, because it really hurt me when he said, 'hike up that dumb mountain' and all that. I learned in psychology class that when someone gets angry it just means they care. But I wasn't thinking about psychology; I was just hurt."

Kim folded her arms in the cold. "I know what you mean. In class I can handle any situation, but when it's real, when it's happening, it's hard to remember exactly what to do."

"He looked the same, Kim, but he really had changed. I

mean, his hair was as dark and curly as ever, and his Adam's apple still stuck out; but when he was mad and bitter like that there was just something I wasn't prepared to cope with. He wasn't the same guy who had thrown peas across the lunchroom with me. We used to sit on the floor in English and laugh about where we might be called on our missions. But then, we were standing in that same English classroom, and he wasn't laughing. He was mad."

Kim questioned, "I don't understand how he had been so hurt, or how he had hurt himself badly enough to give up. It's hard to believe someone with so much could settle for so little. Did he say anything else?"

"Yeah, and this is where I really lost him. When he got control of himself he faced me and said, 'You asked me if I would be the person I would want to be.' His voice was harsh and low like a staticky radio. 'Well, now, I'm asking you, Brad, with all your trying and your preaching, will you be the person you want to be?' "

"Probably not," I had answered, "but I'll be trying."

"But why try?" he exploded again.

"To thank God!" I blurted.

"Mrs. Vroman stopped me then. And that's when we stood quietly for so long, as it says in chapter 1. That's when he said, 'Just sign my release.' "

Kim didn't say anything. We stared out of the window at the snow, which was falling a little lighter now. It seemed mixed up to have such a heavy storm this late in the year. Maybe that's why it fit into my life right then, because I was mixed up, too.

If I sort of crossed my eyes, the snowflakes looked like grainy lines in an old silent movie. The incident in Mrs. Vroman's room had been hard to live through when it was happening a year ago, and now it was hard to relive it.

"What would you have said, Kim? How would you have answered?"

She touched my arm. "You kind of answered him — you did answer him!"

"I guess I did. I told him I have to try to reach my goals and better myself because that is the only way to thank

Heavenly Father for abilities, for blessings, for the gospel, for — for life!"

"That's when he said, 'You'll never stop preaching.' And he was right. I told him I'm trying because that's the only way I know to be a full person."

I felt the same frustration of a year before. "Kim," I asked, "why couldn't I phrase what I felt then?" I remembered words I thought I understood stumbling helplessly through the wet night outside my mind, crawling, whimpering, engulfed in darkness. It seemed as though my feelings would have echoed across towering mountains and filled entire valleys, but where were the words to express them?

"Kim, where were the words?" I leaned my forehead against the metal-cold steering wheel. Except for several errant flakes, the snow had stopped.

Kim pulled the manuscript from its envelope, and after a few moments began reading almost to herself, " 'It costs so much to be a full human being that there are very few who have the enlightenment or the courage to pay the price. . . . The price,' " she repeated. "That's trying."

Here were the words. Here was the answer. I lifted my head to meet Kim's warm smile.

"One has to reach out to the risk of living with both arms. One has to embrace the world like a lover."

I felt tears forming behind my eyes. Tears of relief, childlike tears of joy.

"Embrace the world," I whispered, "like a lover."

BRAD WILCOX'S
TEN TOTAL BARUBA
SUPREME TRYING STEPS

---

1. Praying

2. Making a Value Judgment

3. Doing the Right Thing for the Right Reasons: Multi-Motives

4. Being Self-Motivated

5. Using Your Positive Attitude

6. Acting, Not Reacting

7. Making a Commitment

8. Working

9. Working Together

10. Checking Up